FUNDAMENTALS

OF

ENGLISH GRAMMAR

AND

COMPOSITION

WORKBOOK

by

E. Darrell Holley, Ph.D.

© 2008 by E. Darrell Holley, Ph.D.

Published by Randall House
114 Bush Road
Nashville, TN 37217

All Scripture quotations are taken from The Holy Bible, King James Version.

Printed in the United States of America

10-ISBN 089265581X
13-ISBN 9780892655816

Exercise 1: Verbs and Subjects

Underline the verbs twice and the subjects once.

1. Beowulf destroyed Grendel and delivered the land from the monster.

2. Eventually, Beowulf became the king of the Geats himself.

3. The stalwart hero reigned over his realm for fifty years.

4. Later, the nation was troubled by a terrible dragon.

5. Beowulf killed the dragon, but he himself was killed in the process.

6. The Old English saga depicts Beowulf as a great hero and presents him as the redeemer of his people.

7. Are you familiar with any other ancient Norse sagas?

8. In the twentieth century, Tolkien was inspired by them.

9. There are few literary works of the Anglo-Saxons still in existence.

10. In this book are several passages from the poetry of Caedmon.

11. Anglo-Saxon literature is filled with great heroes, but it is not silent about the ineffable tragedies of human life.

12. For a serious look at ancient English literature, read Tolkien's article about the role of the monsters.

13. The Green Knight strode into Arthur's hall in Camelot.

14. Sir Gawain struck off the Green Knight's head, but the apparition picked up his head, set it back on his shoulders, and rode out.

15. One year later, young Gawain went in search of the Green Knight.

16. Such noble pilgrimages as those of Beowulf and Gawain are a common part of our heroic literature.

17. Chaucer describes a host of characters on a pilgrimage to Canterbury.

18. The knight in Chaucer's *Tales* reminds his listeners of their status as pilgrims.

19. Doesn't Chaucer's parson describe the ultimate destiny of our pilgrimage as "the celestial Jerusalem"?

20. The saints of old considered themselves "strangers and pilgrims on the earth."

21. In Bunyan's famous work, Faithful is martyred in the city of Vanity Fair.

22. At the end of *The Pilgrim's Progress* is a description of Christian's arrival in the Celestial City.

23. Consider the humorous adventures of Mole, Badger, Rat, and Toad in *The Wind in the Willows,* a children's classic.

24. As in a medieval beast fable, the characters take on human characteristics.

Exercise 2: Verbs and Subjects

Underline the verbs twice and the subjects once.

1. Worker bees gather nectar from flowers and carry it back to their hives.

2. The mustangs of the American West are descended from the horses of the Spanish conquistadors.

3. Isn't okra a member of the hibiscus family?

4. There are twenty-two letters in the Hebrew alphabet.

5. The festival of Hanukkah, in the winter, celebrates the victory of the Jews over a pagan tyrant; it is commemmorated by the lighting of the eight-branched menorah.

6. On the veranda stood his father and uncle.

7. The traditional English concept of personal liberty was bolstered by the development of habeas corpus, a legal defense against wrongful imprisonment.

8. Rich farmland covers about three fourths of Hungary and is one of the country's most important natural resources.

9. High blood pressure is a serious condition and can lead to heart attacks, strokes, and kidney failure.

10. A breakfast of eggs, sausage, and grits awaited the hunters upon their return.

11. In spring the hawthorn blooms, and the English countryside turns white.

12. Approximately three fourths of English words are derived, ultimately, from Latin.

13. Skilled calligraphers in monasteries meticulously copied ancient Biblical and classical works.

14. The American opossum, just like the Australian kangaroo, is a marsupial.

15. The oxen groaned in the yoke.

16. A fox slipped into the chicken coop and carried off two hens.

17. During a solar eclipse the shadow of the moon hides the sun from our view.

18. Earth's shadow falls on the moon and creates a lunar eclipse.

19. Earthworms break down the humus in the soil and help the growth of plants.

20. The San Francisco Earthquake of 1906 and the accompanying fire destroyed the city and took many lives.

21. Etymology is the study of the origin and development of words.

22. The area between the Tigris and Euphrates Rivers was exceptionally fertile.

23. In the Middle Ages Oxford and Cambridge Universities were founded in Britain.

Exercise 3: Verbs and Subjects

Underline the verbs twice and the subjects once.

1. Here are the files of all the applicants, Mrs. Priestley.

2. A good resume will provide a potential employer with information about your education, your work experience, and your references.

3. Skills necessary for carpentry, plumbing, and other trades may be acquired through apprenticeships or trade schools.

4. The skills of the learned vocations, including law and medicine, are usually obtained during graduate-level education.

5. Good references will vouch for the applicant's education, skills, experience, or character.

6. What should you wear for a job interview?

7. Employment agencies can provide information about job openings and application procedures.

8. Unfortunately, after three weeks of interviews I had still not found a job, so I was getting depressed.

9. After graduation with a degree in accounting, my brother became a merchant banker in Charleston.

10. Is an undergraduate education sufficient for a career in the ministry?

11. In seminary a young minister will study Biblical languages and theology, as well as pastoral counseling and oratory.

12. Joel did his internship at a hospital in Atlanta and his residency at a hospital in Nashville.

13. There were several positions available with their company.

14. Community colleges frequently offer classes in vocational subjects such as automobile mechanics and appliance repair.

15. Stephen completed his doctoral studies in psychology at Chapel Hill.

16. During the interview she was asked several questions about her previous teaching experience.

17. Was the editor in his office?

18. An architect designs the building and prepares blueprints for the builders.

19. Always give a day's work for a day's pay.

20. Young lawyers frequently serve as clerks for experienced judges; in this way they learn the legal profession from the inside out.

21. Agricultural methods may be studied from books but are best learned on the farm.

22. The nursing students at Aquinas College study both medicine and medical ethics.

Exercise 4: Action Verbs and Linking Verbs

Underline the verbs twice and the subjects once.
Above each verb identify it as an action verb (AV) or a linking verb (LV).

1. During the storm the children remained quite calm.

2. Have you finished your research paper yet?

3. The immigrants had been in the country for only a few months.

4. They had not contemplated the possible outcome of their actions.

5. How long has he been singing in the college choir?

6. Be present at five o'clock sharp.

7. I don't feel very good.

8. These timber-frame buildings were held together with large wooden pegs.

9. Sometimes, settlers built chimneys out of sticks and mud rather than brick or stone.

10. The cabinet-maker turned the wood on the lathe by means of a foot pedal.

11. The New Testament books were written in Koine Greek, the language of the common people.

12. The applesauce on the stove certainly smelled delicious.

13. Anna and Laura had been studying in the library since lunch.

14. As a part-time job I mow the yards and trim the hedges at the college.

15. Before then, I had never written any poetry.

16. The physician felt of my arm and immediately pronounced it broken.

17. No, peaches will not grow well this far north.

18. The yearlings quickly grew fat on the lush grass.

19. Eric looks pale today.

20. Where would I find the periodicals?

21. Read this article and write a two-page summary of it.

22. She would have been excellent for that job, but unfortunately she did not apply for it.

23. Look into the microscope and observe the ameba; then draw a diagram of it.

24. Through years of hard work, persecution, and even imprisonment, the apostle remained true to Christ.

Exercise 5: Predicate Nominatives

Underline the verbs twice and the subjects once.
Circle each predicate nominative and write PN above it.

1. George Washington was the commander-in-chief of the Continental Army.

2. Voters must have been residents of the state for at least six months.

3. How do you become a member of the Daughters of the American Revolution?

4. He remained a patient at the hospital for several weeks.

5. The senator is now the presumptive presidential nominee of his party.

6. Are Don and Stephanie the new class officers?

7. Most of the early settlers of the Carolinas were immigrants from England.

8. Paul became a Christian on the road to Damascus.

9. Has he always been an avid NASCAR fan?

10. Thy Word is a lamp unto my feet and a light unto my path. —Psalm 119:105

11. The little city of Rome became the conqueror of the Western world.

12. Is Luxembourg or Malta the smallest member of the European Union?

13. Miguel de Cervantes is the most important author of all Spanish literature.

14. Wasn't Jefferson the author of the Declaration of Independence?

15. James Fenimore Cooper's most famous character is Natty Bumppo or Leatherstocking.

16. Robinson Crusoe remained a castaway on the island for over twenty years.

17. Plato was the author of numerous dialogues about questions of morality and philosophy.

18. Mr. Pinson became president of the college at the young age of thirty-five.

19. C. S. Lewis is one of the most well-known Christian apologists of the twentieth century.

20. How could Benedict Arnold have been a traitor to Washington and the patriot cause?

21. Without a scholarship he cannot remain a student at the university.

22. The Phoenicians may have been the creators of the alphabet.

23. My sister is a high-school librarian in an inner-city school in Chicago.

24. Will Dr. Reid be the editor of the entire series of Biblical commentaries?

25. You seem a happier person today.

Exercise 6: Predicate Adjectives

Underline the verbs twice and the subjects once.
Circle each predicate adjective and write PA above it.

1. The etouffe, with vegetables, sausage, shrimp, and peppers, tasted very spicy.

2. The change of the guard at Buckingham Palace is magnificent.

3. The bridge over the gorge, though old, still seemed reliable.

4. Are they ready yet?

5. The surface of the old table was smooth from years of use.

6. Monticello, inspired by Jefferson's visit to Europe, is classical in design.

7. The odd kiwi fruit is brown, fuzzy, and egg-shaped, but it tastes delicious, much like a strawberry.

8. Something in the refrigerator smells rancid.

9. The residents of the area seemed very upset about the proposed zoning changes.

10. I am sorry, but I have grown weary of his excuses.

11. Despite all our attempts at drainage, that field remains much too wet for corn.

12. The pickup truck has stayed popular despite higher gasoline prices.

13. The children had been cranky all day.

14. Japan remained isolated from the West until 1853.

15. Aren't azaleas and rhododendrons similar in appearance?

16. The cabins of the early settlers were generally small, with few windows.

17. She was, unfortunately, blind and deaf from birth.

18. The coat of the Irish setter may be solid red or red with white markings.

19. The nation of Israel has been independent only since 1948.

20. Does this soup taste salty to you?

21. With children, the English setter is calm, affectionate, and patient.

22. Until the advent of modern plumbing, the daily bath was unknown.

23. The peasants in Pieter Bruegel's paintings appear stocky and coarse and almost comical.

24. Each Brussels sprout looks similar to a tiny head of cabbage.

25. How are honey bees and bumble bees different?

Exercise 7: Predicate Nominatives and Predicate Adjectives

Underline the verbs twice and the subjects once.
Circle each complement and write PN (predicate nominative) or PA (predicate adjective) above it.

1. Most Icelanders are descendants of Viking settlers.

2. After over seventy years of totalitarian rule, the Soviet Union became nonexistent in December, 1991.

3. Tobacco remained the primary money-making crop of Kentucky for many years.

4. How successful were their voter-registration efforts?

5. *Gulliver's Travels*, though containing many elements of adventure and fantasy, is not a children's story at all; it was a satirical look at contemporary British life.

6. The gingko, first discovered in temple gardens in China, has become a common urban lawn tree in the United States.

7. The human figures in the sculptures of Giacometti seem lonely and alienated from one another.

8. In feudal society, everyone except perhaps the king was someone else's vassal.

9. The correspondence between John Adams and his wife Abigail is romantic, witty, and lively.

10. Modernist buildings are generally cubelike and devoid of decoration; to many people they appear quite ugly.

11. For thousands of years, oxen had been the primary draft animals on farms.

12. The population of Australia is extremely small in relation to the nation's huge size.

13. The number of deaths from automobile accidents each year is shocking.

14. Atlanta became a center of commerce because of its access to railroads.

15. In the second half of the twentieth century, William F. Buckley became one of the most well-known spokesmen for political conservatism in the United States.

16. Two musical techniques characteristic of Bach are counterpoint and the fugue.

17. The piano did not become a popular instrument until the nineteenth century.

18. The sound of the horns seemed inappropriate in the composition.

19. Maryland remained a haven for English Catholics throughout the early colonial period.

20. Checking and savings accounts are not the only services provided in banks.

21. The interest on loans is the main source of income for banks.

22. According to many baseball fans, the idea of a designated hitter is ridiculous and ruinous to the nature of the sport.

23. The piccolo sounds quite high in pitch, but the bassoon is quite low.

24. The birds depicted by Audubon are amazingly detailed and accurate.

25. Residents of the coastal community remained unaware of the approaching storm.

Exercise 8: Direct Objects

Underline the verbs twice and the subjects once.
Circle each direct object and write DO above it.

1. Oliver Goldsmith wrote an important poem and an important novel.

2. In "The Deserted Village" Goldsmith discusses some of the problems of farm life in his day.

3. His novel describes the life of a rural clergyman and his family.

4. Had not Goliath threatened the armies of Israel day after day?

5. Several senators proposed a fifteen-percent tax cut, but the president opposed it.

6. In 55 BC Julius Caesar brought Roman troops into Britain for the first time.

7. Later, various Germanic tribes also invaded the island.

8. King Arthur established his capital at Camelot.

9. King Alfred united the seven Anglo-Saxon kingdoms and made peace with the Danes.

10. The mariners smelled the brisk salt air.

11. Have you ever tasted steak and kidney pie?

12. Her brother is attending a university in Connecticut.

13. The visiting speaker addressed the class on the subject of business ethics.

14. In the Old Testament the prophets frequently warn Israel about the dangers of idolatry.

15. Despite our three quilts, we could still feel the bitter cold.

16. James VI of Scotland, the cousin of Elizabeth, succeeded her upon her death in 1603.

17. Sir William Blackstone's *Commentaries on the Laws of England* educated Englishmen and Americans about the English common law.

18. Only in the early seventeenth century did physicians understand the circulation of the blood throughout the body.

19. His dentist recommended the removal of the abcessed tooth.

20. The boa constrictor crushes its victims and then swallows them.

21. In the Peloponnesian War Athens and her allies fought Sparta and her allies.

22. Pine straw makes an excellent mulch, but it may increase the acidity of the soil.

23. In the art of bonsai, a gardener produces a miniature tree with all the characteristics of a large tree in nature.

24. The Arts and Crafts Movement in the nineteenth century emphasized the connections of usefulness and beauty in domestic objects such as furniture and fabrics.

25. The first baseman caught the ball and threw it to the second baseman for a double play.

Exercise 9: Direct Objects

Underline the verbs twice and the subjects once.
Circle each direct object and write DO above it.

1. The ancient Egyptians made paper from the stems of the papyrus.

2. Hebrews, Greeks, and other ancient peoples used parchment scrolls for government and business records as well as for literary and religious documents.

3. Eventually, copyists bound pieces of parchment together into books.

4. In the Middle Ages, expert illuminators created beautiful, colorful designs and illustrations for manuscripts.

5. Chinese inventors devised the process for the production of paper from wood fibers.

6. How did they print things without movable type?

7. Johannes Gutenberg and his associates developed the modern printing press.

8. William Caxton set up the first modern printing press in England in 1477.

9. In 1525, William Tyndale produced the first printed English New Testament.

10. The printers of the Geneva Bible introduced maps to the Biblical text.

11. About seven years after his death, the *First Folio* collected most of Shakespeare's works.

12. Though produced by a committee, the King James Bible achieved an admirable beauty and grace.

13. In the Middle Ages, elementary schools taught only the Latin language.

14. However, with the Renaissance and the increase in the production of English books, the schools began the systematic instruction of the vernacular.

15. Chapmen or peddlers sold cheap paperback books from village to village.

16. Many children learned their letters from a hand-held hornbook.

17. The Puritans published *The Bay Psalm Book* in colonial Massachusetts.

18. Who set up the first printing press in America?

19. The introduction of cloth covers rather than leather covers reduced the price of books.

20. The linotype machine set type mechanically rather than by hand.

21. Many collectors desire first editions of certain books or books with the authors' autographs or copies with the original dust jackets.

22. Will the computer increase or decrease the importance of printed books?

23. Our public library contains numerous books in braille for the use of the blind.

24. Have scholars located all the original manuscripts of Shakespeare's plays?

25. Printers have given unusual names to the different type fonts.

Exercise 10: Direct Objects and Indirect Objects

Underline the verbs twice and the subjects once.
Circle each direct object and write DO above it.
Circle each indirect object and write IO above it.

1. I sent my girlfriend a bouquet of roses for her birthday.

2. Teachers will give the students a syllabus with the requirements of the course and a list of textbooks.

3. Mrs. Grimes made her family an apple pie.

4. The receptionist handed Kathleen an employment application form.

5. Did she give her research paper an appropriate amount of time?

6. Mr. Carter read his American history class some selections from speeches of Patrick Henry.

7. During my trip to Canada, I mailed my friends several postcards.

8. Did you give a copy of this pamphlet to the dean?

9. After his critical illness and extended hospital stay, Bob owed the hospital $50,000.

10. Did you tell your father that funny story about Kevin?

11. True religion affords government its surest support. —George Washington

12. Which constitutional amendment gave women the vote?

13. Their business's location provides it a great deal of walk-in business.

14. In the play *Our Town* Thornton Wilder gives his audience a lesson on the significance of everyday life.

15. The three witches told Macbeth things about his future.

16. Mayor Purcell presented the students certificates of appreciation for their contributions to the betterment of the city.

17. Sitting on the front porch, Andy played Sarah several songs on his guitar.

18. Unfortunately, he did not tell her the truth.

19. Actually, this situation affords us the opportunity of a new beginning.

20. These candidates offer us very different platforms.

21. President Monroe sent the Europeans a warning about further colonization in the Western Hemisphere.

22. This collection of the letters of John and Abigail Adams gives readers a rare look at their personal relationship.

23. John Harvard left the college a collection of books and a gift of money.

24. The historical works of Josephus have given scholars much background information about first-century life in Palestine.

25. The surgical nurse handed the surgeon a pair of forceps.

Exercise 11: Direct Objects and Indirect Objects

Underline the verbs twice and the subjects once.
Circle each direct object and write DO above it.
Circle each indirect object and write IO above it.

1. Friends, Romans, countrymen, lend me your ears. —William Shakespeare

2. The prime minister granted the reporters of the London newspapers a special interview.

3. On my graduation day, my uncle in Mobile gave me a set of encyclopedias.

4. After our comments, our mother gave Addie and me a look of disapproval.

5. Dr. Snowden showed his students several examples of igneous, sedimentary, and metamorphic rocks.

6. Several local property owners have deeded the state nine hundred acres of virgin forest.

7. Offer a cow a nutmeg, and she will reject it for old hay. —Martin Luther

8. After the couple's marriage vows, their pastor preached them a short homily on the duties of husbands and wives.

9. Send your suggestions or questions to the station manager.

10. Citizens should give their elected representatives their opinions about matters of importance to them.

11. My cousin in Italy mailed me several photographs of his children.

12. Give the garden some attention as soon as possible: clip the hedges and give the roses some mulch.

13. The letters of the Paston family cover several decades and give scholars a first-hand view of medieval cultural life.

14. The ushers handed everyone a copy of the program.

15. In *Don Quixote* Cervantes was giving his fellow Spaniards a humorous look at the reign of Philip II.

16. Ralph's mechanic told him the bad news: the truck needed a whole new transmission.

17. The dean of students announced the outcome of the election to the students.

18. Our neighbors offered Alice and me some rutabagas and turnips from their garden.

19. Did you prepare Dr. Thomas a list of all your current medications?

20. An alumnus left the college a collection of over seven hundred books, most of them about archaeology.

21. In her speech, Jenna gave the students five reasons for the adoption of the constitutional amendment.

22. Allan sent his girlfriend several love poems.

23. *The Federalist Papers* gave Americans a defense of the new federal constitution.

24. In the last scene of the play, Kate gives the audience a lecture on marriage.

25. The rejection of moral absolutes by many people presents us a major obstacle.

Exercise 12: Direct Objects and Objective Complements

Underline the verbs twice and the subjects once.
Circle each direct object and write DO above it.
Circle each objective complement and write OC above it.

1. The thirteenth amendment declared slavery illegal.

2. Wally and Linda named the unfortunate child Wallenda.

3. The library makes newspapers from around the country available in the second-floor reading room.

4. Our victory at the forensics tournament certainly made us happy.

5. Marie found the soup too salty for her taste.

6. The students elected Ryan student-body president by an overwhelming majority.

7. The school board made Mr. Howard the new elementary supervisor.

8. The speaker of the House considers the new tax bill unwise.

9. Most members of the jury considered the defendent guilty.

10. Did you find the article helpful in your research?

11. Do you consider him honest and reliable?

12. I thought the judge's comments very inappropriate for an officer of the court.

13. He had always considered Imogene the most beautiful and most intelligent woman in the world.

14. Our next-door neighbors painted their house pink.

15. The girls on the softball team made Theresa their captain.

16. She dyed the wool blue.

17. The shareholders elected Harrison chief executive officer of the company.

18. The cold temperatures affect the sugars in the plants' leaves and turn them yellow and orange and red.

19. Before its fateful maiden voyage, newspapers had declared the *Titanic* unsinkable.

20. In the "roaring '20s," many young women threw off tradition and cut their hair short.

21. Why did Conrad name the work *Heart of Darkness*?

22. The anesthesia immediately made him sleepy.

23. These Macedonians call a spade a spade. —Plutarch

24. Lower interest rates will make capital less available for loans.

25. Dost thou call me a fool, boy? —William Shakespeare

Exercise 13: Direct Objects and Objective Complements

Underline the verbs twice and the subjects once.
Circle each direct object and write DO above it.
Circle each objective complement and write OC above it.

1. Abraham named the place Jehovah-jireh ("the Lord will provide").
2. Of all your classes, which do you find the most interesting?
3. The judge pronounced the defendent not guilty and adjourned the court.
4. The recent drought has left the fields parched and dry.
5. Hamlet found his mother alone in her chamber and spoke to her.
6. The judges at the Nuremburg Trials declared the Nazis' actions indefensible.
7. Paleontologists called the extinct reptiles dinosaurs ("terrible lizards").
8. Mr. Darcy's sharp words made Elizabeth Bennet quite angry.
9. Robert Herrick, the poet of the English West Country, entitled his poems *The Hesperides* after the Western nymphs of Greek mythology.
10. Bernice inadvertantly dyed her hair green.
11. The difficulties and privations of his youth left the boy wary and hesitant, but they also made him strong and persistent.
12. The horns on the head of pentaceratops must have made him particularly fearsome to his enemies.
13. The AIDS virus renders the immune system ineffective and leaves the patient susceptible to any and every pathogen.
14. In the 1948 presidential election they dubbed the States' Rights Party the "Dixiecrats."
15. Because of the dogs' origin in Spain, breeders called them spaniels.
16. The many classical, mythological, and Biblical allusions in Milton's *Paradise Lost* as well as the complex sentence structure have made it very difficult for most modern readers.
17. On his voyage of discovery, Sir Francis Drake landed on the Pacific Coast near present-day San Francisco and named the area New Albion.
18. Drake's voyage around the globe made him famous and brought him praise from Queen Elizabeth.
19. Two presidents have been impeached; the Senate found both not guilty.
20. Did Bach himself call these pieces *The Goldberg Variations* or did others call them that later?
21. Their weak branches make these trees liable to considerable damage during strong winds.
22. Did you find the roast beef tough also?
23. In his novel about modern religious apostasy, Thomas Hardy appropriately names his protagonist Jude Fawley.
24. Does the evidence of earlier Viking settlements in North America render the previous hypotheses obsolete?

Exercise 14: Indirect Objects and Objective Complements

Underline the verbs twice and the subjects once.
Circle each direct object and write DO above it.
Circle each indirect object and write IO above it.
Circle each objective complement and write OC above it.

1. Tom Lea's painting gives the viewer a glimpse of the privations in the American South after the end of the Civil War.

2. The Supreme Court declared the law unconstitutional.

3. Mrs. Rood gave the students a test on the bones in the human skeleton.

4. China calls itself a republic, but it does not give its citizens any choice in elections.

5. Raleigh named his colony Virginia after Queen Elizabeth, "the Virgin Queen."

6. The use of dovetail joints makes a piece of furniture stronger and thus more durable.

7. The question of human freedom and divine sovereignty has given theologians and philosophers considerable trouble.

8. Calvinists consider God's choices concerning man's salvation unconditional.

9. According to Arminians, God has given man free will.

10. Rhode Island's religious toleration made it an attractive haven for both Jews and Baptists.

11. The wooden stock gives the rifle stability and keeps it steady.

12. German gunsmiths in Pennsylvania made the colonial rifle much more accurate.

13. Give today's speaker your undivided attention.

14. How can you cast your vote for a person with those views?

15. Its strong fibers give sisal toughness and make it ideal for floor covering.

16. The students found the instructions unclear and therefore asked their teacher numerous questions.

17. The smorgasbord offered the diners a tempting array of various dishes.

18. The hurricane left hundreds of people homeless.

19. All the different colors and styles gave me too many options.

20. One of his assistants handed the president an urgent message.

21. Years of over-cultivation have left the land barren and lifeless.

22. My lawyer sent me a letter with the details of the agreement.

23. The president appointed him ambassador to Poland.

24. Mrs. Pinson and the other faculty wives offered us some delightful refreshments.

25. South Carolinians elected Strom Thurmond senator over and over again.

Exercise 15: Indirect Objects and Objective Complements

Underline the verbs twice and the subjects once.
Circle each direct object and write DO above it.
Circle each indirect object and write IO above it.
Circle each objective complement and write OC above it.

1. Actually, the treatments made him sicker.

2. In mercantilist policy, the European countries considered their colonies merely sources of raw material and customers for their manufactured goods.

3. After a review of his education and experience and after a thorough interview, the board of trustees elected him president of the college.

4. The old man had left his children the best inheritance possible, a good example.

5. The doctor prescribed him three different medications.

6. Who taught you that poem?

7. The boys on the ladders handed the roofers additional shingles.

8. Keep me informed about the results of the experiment.

9. Because of his overuse of credit cards, he now owes his creditors thousands of dollars.

10. Throw me another pillow.

11. I sent the publisher a copy of my manuscript.

12. Britain's isolation always afforded it a measure of separation from the affairs of Europe.

13. James Herriot's years as a veterinarian in Yorkshire provided him a wealth of material for his books.

14. Which of Monet's paintings do the critics generally consider his best?

15. Study of a foreign language frequently makes a student more knowledgeable about his own.

16. Divine grace sets man free from his bondage to sin.

17. Why does the Hebrew proverb call beauty "vain" and "deceitful"?

18. Robinson Crusoe named his savage companion Friday.

19. The House allots its members a certain amount of time for debate, but the Senate gives its members no limits.

20. Give every man thy ear, but few thy voice. —William Shakespeare

21. After her poor grade on the first test, Diana gave her calculus class more time.

22. The Agrarian writers of the 1930s declared modernity spiritually bankrupt and offered the nation a contrasting view of success.

23. In *The Great Gatsby* F. Scott Fitzgerald also offers his readers a decidedly negative view of the "American dream."

24. Corrie ten Boom and her family provided their Jewish neighbors a safe hiding place.

25. I sent my representative a letter with my objections to the bill.

Exercise 16: Retained Objects

Underline the verbs twice and the subjects once.
Identify each transitive passive action verb by writing TP above it.
Circle each retained object and write RO above it.

1. We were given these "unalienable rights" by God Himself.

2. The young couple were given some interesting wedding gifts.

3. She was given a bracelet by her mother.

4. Was this farm left you by your grandfather?

5. In my opinion, the murderer was rightly given the death penalty.

6. Veterans of the Revolutionary War were granted homesteads in the new territories.

7. In Christ's parable, each of the stewards is allotted a certain number of talents.

8. The children in the one-room school were taught reading, writing, and arithmetic.

9. He was denied the opportunity of a response to the accusations.

10. We were given incorrect information on the telephone.

11. Was sufficient time given them for completion of the project?

12. On the Lupercal, Julius Caesar was thrice offered a crown by Marc Antony.

13. Was the academic dean given a copy of your course syllabus?

14. Yes, this was told me by my brother.

15. The winners in the area of animal husbandry were awarded blue ribbons by the judges.

16. Each candidate was allotted five minutes for a short campaign speech.

17. The Holy Child was presented gifts of gold, frankincense, and myrrh.

18. Under no conditions will any additional funds be given them.

19. Was any compromise or accommodation offered them?

20. I have just been handed an important announcement.

21. The story was told me in this manner.

22. In 1660 the son of the late king was offered the throne.

23. The good news was given the shepherds by heralding angels.

24. In the summer, any unwary person will be given even more squash by his neighbors.

25. William Faulkner was awarded a Pulitzer Prize in 1963 for *The Reivers*.

Exercise 17: Direct Objects, Indirect Objects, and Retained Objects

Underline the verbs twice and the subjects once.
Identify each verb by writing TA (transitive active action verb) or TP (transitive passive action verb) above it.
Circle each complement and identify it by writing above it DO (direct object), IO (indirect object), or RO (retained object).

1. The library was given a page from a medieval manuscript.

2. A good time was had by all.

3. Has the matter been given enough attention?

4. In the beginning God created the heaven and the earth. —Genesis 1:1

5. A brief leave of absence was granted the soldier because of a family emergency.

6. Only Daniel could read the handwriting on the wall.

7. Has the grand jury been given this evidence?

8. The ploughman homeward plods his weary way and leaves the world to darkness and to me.

    —Thomas Gray

9. The Dutch reportedly paid the Indians $24 for Manhattan Island.

10. Earlier, a key had been given him, and with it Christian could unlock the door of Doubting Castle.

11. The children's father gave them bicycles for Christmas.

12. Joel has been awarded a merit badge in archery.

13. Late in life, Shakespeare built himself a new home in Stratford.

14. Did you give the department secretary a copy of your schedule?

15. I was bequeathed these leather-bound travel books by my uncle, a lawyer in Cincinatti.

16. I handed the state trooper my driver's license.

17. The study of the English language was given a huge impetus by the publication of the English Bible in the sixteenth and seventeenth centuries.

18. Upon his retirement, the faculty gave Mr. Malone a beautiful mantel clock.

19. By federal law, one hundred sixty acres could be allotted each homesteader.

20. The Linnaean classification system assigns a specific Latin name to each plant or animal.

21. Her brother has been awarded an appointment to the U. S. Military Academy at West Point.

22. Due to his injuries, the soldier was given an honorable discharge from the army.

23. Give us a summary of *King Lear.*

24. The carpenter's assistant handed him the miter square.

25. After a review of her needs assessment form, Ruth Ann was awarded additional financial aid.

Exercise 18: Prepositions

Write Yes if the word can be used as a preposition and No if it cannot.

_____	1.	throughout	_____	26.	what
_____	2.	among	_____	27.	often
_____	3.	are	_____	28.	amid
_____	4.	because of	_____	29.	up
_____	5.	past	_____	30.	by
_____	6.	persuade	_____	31.	though
_____	7.	during	_____	32.	beneath
_____	8.	and	_____	33.	or
_____	9.	instead of	_____	34.	into
_____	10.	except	_____	35.	even
_____	11.	accept	_____	36.	like
_____	12.	out of	_____	37.	down
_____	13.	since	_____	38.	at
_____	14.	although	_____	39.	can
_____	15.	between	_____	40.	must
_____	16.	across	_____	41.	early
_____	17.	according to	_____	42.	him
_____	18.	toward	_____	43.	sometimes
_____	19.	with	_____	44.	behind
_____	20.	before	_____	45.	after
_____	21.	for	_____	46.	above
_____	22.	until	_____	47.	theirs
_____	23.	underneath	_____	48.	there
_____	24.	when	_____	49.	unto
_____	25.	how	_____	50.	regardless of

Exercise 19: Prepositional Phrases

Underline the verbs twice and the subjects once.
Label all complements (PN, PA, DO, IO, OC, RO).
Put parentheses around all prepositional phrases.

1. Unto Him be glory in the church by Christ Jesus throughout all ages. —Ephesians 3:21

2. In spite of the summer hailstorm, the farmer salvaged a third of his wheat crop.

3. I cried unto the Lord with my voice, and He heard me out of His holy hill. —Psalm 3:4

4. American settlers crossed over the Alleghenies prior to the Revolutionary War.

5. Thousands in Hannibal's armies perished on the slopes of the Alps.

6. All the gods of the nations are idols, but the Lord made the heavens. —Psalm 96:5

7. He escaped out of their hand and went away again beyond Jordan. —John 10:39

8. He leadeth me in the paths of righteousness for His name's sake. —Psalm 23:3

9. Love looks not with the eyes but with the mind. —William Shakespeare

10. The devil can cite Scripture for his purpose. —William Shakespeare

11. I would not have given it for a wilderness of monkeys. —William Shakespeare

12. The quality of mercy is not strained; it droppeth as the gentle rain from heaven upon the place
    beneath. —William Shakespeare

13. I will follow thee to the last gasp with truth and loyalty. —William Shakespeare

14. For God's sake, let us sit upon the ground and tell sad stories of the death of kings.
    —William Shakespeare

15. My crown is in my heart, not on my head, not decked with diamonds and Indian stones.
    —William Shakespeare

16. According to the old story, the sailors listened to the call of the Lorelei and were wrecked upon the
    rocks.

17. At the conclusion of the play, the actors stood behind the curtain and waited for their final bow.

18. Poor Lazarus lay at the rich man's gate and desired the crumbs from his table.

19. In front of the travellers stood the mountains, but beyond those mountains was a vast, fertile plain.

20. The door opened onto a tube-shaped hall like a tunnel: a very comfortable tunnel without smoke, with
    panelled walls and floors tiled and carpeted, provided with polished chairs and lots and lots of pegs for
    hats and coats. —J. R. R. Tolkien

21. As the frontispiece of the book, the author has used an engraving by Durer.

22. At once a voice arose among the bleak twigs overhead in a full-hearted evensong of joy illimited.
    —Thomas Hardy

23. We crossed the river on a narrow wooden bridge.

24. After class several students asked the teacher about the assignment.

Exercise 20: Prepositions and Adverbs

In the blank at the left tell whether the italicized word is used as a preposition (PREP) or as an adverb (ADV). If the italicized word is used as a preposition, put parentheses around the entire prepositional phrase.

_____ 1. Everybody, soon or late, sits *down* to a banquet of consequences.

—Robert Louis Stevenson

_____ 2. Moses went back *down* the mountain to the camp of Israel.

_____ 3. We are more than conquerors *through* Him. —Romans 8:37

_____ 4. A city bus should be coming *along* at any moment.

_____ 5. Pirates once hid *along* the Barbary Coast of northern Africa.

_____ 6. He slowly made his way *up* the narrow staircase.

_____ 7. The hunter looked *up* and saw a wild turkey in a pine tree.

_____ 8. The pioneers traveled *over* the Rocky Mountains toward California.

_____ 9. The tree suddenly gave way and fell *over*.

_____ 10. They left *behind* most of their furniture and other household possessions.

_____ 11. I climbed *aboard* and found a seat near the back of the car.

_____ 12. *Within* a few minutes, a loud alarm bell sounded.

_____ 13. Of all the sailors *aboard* the ship, Queequeg was certainly the strangest.

_____ 14. My former enemy strode *across* the room and took my hand in his.

_____ 15. Suddenly, bullets whizzed *past* with alarming consequences.

_____ 16. We sailed *across* and found them on the opposite shore.

_____ 17. It was long past noon, but no one had shown *up* yet.

_____ 18. *Within* were the rest of my family, safe and sound.

_____ 19. From the hive thousands of bees flew *out* and swarmed around me.

_____ 20. Come in out of the cold and sit *beside* the fire.

_____ 21. We edged our way *along* the steep slope, trying not to fall.

_____ 22. The other disciples fled, but John stood *near* and watched the proceedings.

_____ 23. As we walked *along*, we talked.

_____ 24. I hung *on* for dear life.

_____ 25. *Near* the edge of town was a small house with a green door.

Exercise 21: Prepositional Phrases

Underline the verbs twice and the subjects once.
Label all complements (PN, PA, DO, IO, OC, RO).
Put parentheses around all prepositional phrases.
Draw an arrow to the word that the prepositional phrase modifies.
Above the prepositional phrase tell whether the prepositional phrase is used as an adjective (ADJ) or as an adverb (ADV).

1. As for me and my house, we will serve the Lord. —Joshua 24:15

2. Within the concentration camp were thousands of Jewish prisoners.

3. Across the auditorium was a large banner.

4. The geologists have drilled into a layer of shale underneath the harder layer above.

5. After the game our soccer team went to David's house for a victory celebration.

6. During the tremor, items on the store shelves fell onto the floor.

7. In spite of my inexperience, the captain sent me into the game.

8. Amid the confusion of the battle, the soldiers lost their direction.

9. Everyone except for Allan arrived at the wedding on time.

10. Since the development of its oil industry in the mid-1900s, Saudi Arabia has become a wealthy nation.

11. The rings of Saturn go around the planet at its equator.

12. An axis is an imaginary line through a planet's center.

13. According to legend, St. Nicholas would secretly throw bags of money through the windows of the poor.

14. Perhaps because of this tale, throughout history St. Nicholas has been a symbol of charity.

15. Near Salisbury in southern England stands Stonehenge, the largest prehistoric structure in the British Isles.

16. A snake can use its head and tail as supports and thereby lift its body sideways.

17. The snake can thus move across the sand and leave these distinctive sideways tracks behind it.

18. Under the leadership of General Sherman, the Union troops moved through Georgia; terrible civilian devastation followed along the army's path.

19. Sheep are raised around the world for both meat and wool.

20. A dilapidated old cabin without a roof stood beside the road.

21. From the gallery visitors could watch the business on the Senate floor.

22. Within the stomach, the food is churned and mixed with enzymes.

23. During the festival of Sukkot, Jews remember their years in the wilderness of Sinai.

24. On account of the rain, the construction was postponed to next week.

25. Women would make small brooms out of sedge for use in their homes.

Exercise 22: Prepositional Phrases

Underline the verbs twice and the subjects once.
Label all complements (PN, PA, DO, IO, OC, RO).
Put parentheses around all prepositional phrases.
Draw an arrow to the word that the prepositional phrase modifies.
Above the prepositional phrase tell whether the prepositional phrase is used as an adjective (ADJ) or as an adverb (ADV).

1. Young Moses was educated like a prince in the land of Egypt

2. He was brought up in the courts of Pharaoh, but he was no doubt taught in the faith of Abraham by his mother.

3. Saul studied at the feet of the great Hebrew scholar Gamaliel.

4. Because of his excellent education, Saul or Paul was an able defender of the Christian gospel.

5. In conversation with the Athenian philosophers on Mars' Hill, Paul could give a thoughtful and powerful defence of the Christian faith.

6. Johann Sebastian Bach dedicated all of his works "to the glory of God alone."

7. Make a joyful noise unto the Lord, all ye lands. —Psalm 100:1

8. According to this article, John Milton wrote *Paradise Lost* after the onset of his blindness.

9. The story of *Paradise Lost* concerns the fall of man in the Garden of Eden.

10. After his conversion, Francis Schaeffer wrote several works about the growth and decline of Christian civilization in the West.

11. This is another book about the dissolution of the West. —Richard Weaver

12. The defeat of logical realism in the great medieval debate was the crucial event in the history of Western culture. —Richard Weaver

13. According to Weaver, the denial of the reality of universal ideals brings about the rejection of truth.

14. Aristotle had recognized an element of unintelligibility in the world, but the view of nature as a rational mechanism expelled this element. —Richard Weaver

15. During the late nineteenth and early twentieth centuries, such theories as Darwinism and behaviorism rejected the existence of human freedom.

16. The expulsion of the element of unintelligibility in nature was followed by the abandonment of the doctrine of original sin. —Richard Weaver

17. In the modernists' theories man is "beyond freedom and dignity."

18. At the feeder on the window sill, goldfinches, titmice, chickadees, nuthatches, and cardinals have been busy at a heap of free (to them) sunflower seeds. —Wendell Berry

19. We are alive within mystery, by miracle. —Wendell Berry

20. In his dream Richard III is confronted by the ghosts of his victims.

Exercise 23: Principal Parts of Verbs

In the blanks provided give the present participle, the past, and the past participle of each verb.

present	present participle	past	past participle
1. love			
2. write			
3. hurry			
4. drink			
5. eat			
6. judge			
7. buy			
8. steal			
9. cover			
10. think			
11. sing			
12. lose			
13. ride			
14. paint			
15. pray			
16. know			
17. throw			
18. freeze			
19. worry			
20. imagine			
21. speak			
22. rise			
23. strike			
24. lift			
25. fly			

Exercise 24: Participial Phrases

Underline the verbs twice and the subjects once.
Label all complements (PN, PA, DO, IO, OC, RO).
Put a wavy line under the participle.
Put parentheses around the participial phrase.
In the blank at the left write the word that the participial phrase is modifying.

_____ 1. Every kingdom divided against itself is brought to desolation. —Luke 11:17

_____ 2. Abraham saw a ram caught in a thicket by his horns.

_____ 3. Standing on the hilltop, we could see for several miles.

_____ 4. My brother lives in an old home, recently remodeled into apartments.

_____ 5. We hung our dripping clothes on the firescreen.

_____ 6. The permanently frozen ground in arctic regions makes the land a wasteland.

_____ 7. The great number of shirts hanging on the line indicated a large family of boys.

_____ 8. Dolon did not see the warrior hiding behind a clump of bushes.

_____ 9. This phylum is very different from the one composed of arachnids.

_____ 10. Jonathan stared across the room at the beautiful girl talking to his sister.

_____ 11. Unfortunately, the tractor bogged down in the pasture was loaned to me by my neighbor.

_____ 12. The speaker addressing the student body today is an archaeologist.

_____ 13. Regulus, having given his word of honor, returned to the Carthaginian camp.

_____ 14. They first repaired the windows broken in the storm.

_____ 15. Having begun so well, we should not stop now.

_____ 16. In Elizabethan gardens there were frequently flower beds planted in unusual patterns.

_____ 17. Coming around the corner too fast, she lost control of the car.

_____ 18. The gases created by the combustion of the jet fuel rush out with great velocity and create jet thrust.

_____ 19. Many dissidents, severely persecuted in their homelands, sought refuge in the United States.

_____ 20. An apartment, newly repainted and thoroughly cleaned, will be available for you by August 1.

_____ 21. Mr. McKeown, glancing frequently at the clock, gobbled down his breakfast and hurriedly left for his first appointment.

_____ 22. Having pried open the window, the burglar crept silently into the basement.

_____ 23. Looking from the airplane, the governor could see the hurricane's devastation to the land below.

_____ 24. Did you read the label attached to the suit?

_____ 25. Have they recovered all the money stolen in the bank hold-up?

Exercise 25: Participial Phrases

Underline the verbs twice and the subjects once.
Label all complements (PN, PA, DO, IO, OC, RO).
Put a wavy line under the participle.
Put parentheses around the participial phrase.
In the blank at the left write the word that the participial phrase is modifying.

1. The Northwest Territory included the area now containing Ohio, Indiana, Illinois, Michigan, and Wisconsin.

2. Having received land grants for their services in the Revolution, many veterans and their families headed southwest into Alabama, Mississippi, and Florida.

3. A coarse fabric made out of linen and wool was used for most clothes.

4. Cabins built from logs provided shelter for most settlers.

5. Many women made quilts from scraps of fabric sewn together in colorful patterns.

6. Cabbage, having been shredded and stored in salty brine, could be kept for months.

7. In the smokehouse was meat obtained from our own hogs.

8. They might have a few books published in places like Boston or Philadelphia or Charleston.

9. Sensing the need for religious and secular instruction, the settlers quickly established churches and schools.

10. Preachers called circuit riders might arrive only once a month or so.

11. At dances fiddlers played old tunes originating in Britain and Scotland.

12. Wagons pulled by oxen could cover only about twelve to twenty miles per day.

13. Seeing Diana and Robert, I hollered and waved my arms.

14. Do you know the boy standing on the front row in this photograph?

15. Chinese revolutionaries, having overthrown the ineffective Manchu emperors, established the Republic of China in 1912.

16. The noise was coming from a large flock of birds roosting in the apple orchard.

17. Using a lathe, the cabinetmaker shaped the piece of wood into a table leg.

18. The stones pushed along by the movement of the glacier can still be seen in this area.

19. The librarian ordered the books requested by the teachers in the various academic departments.

20. In western China are the Uygurs, a group of people speaking an Indo-European language.

21. The corn, having been stored in the crib, was thus available throughout the winter.

22. Arriving in Athens, Paul went to Mars Hill, the center of Athenian religion and culture.

23. The creature making all the racket was a red-headed woodpecker in a pecan tree.

24. On the return voyage the hulls were filled with rocks put there for ballast.

25. Was the knife hidden in his jacket discovered by the guards?

Exercise 26: Gerund Phrases

Underline the verbs twice and the subjects once.
Label all complements (PN, PA, DO, IO, OC, RO).
Put a wavy line under the gerund.
Put parentheses around the gerund phrase.
In the blank at the left tell how the gerund phrase is used by writing S (subject), PN (predicate nominative), DO (direct object), OP (object of a preposition), etc.

_____	1.	Will the president consider running for a second term?
_____	2.	The magician succeeded in diverting the audience's attention away from his left hand.
_____	3.	Reading the plays aloud will aid in your comprehension.
_____	4.	By asking that question I intended no disrespect, sir.
_____	5.	My grandfather greatly enjoys working in his garden.
_____	6.	Getting into debt can cause you many problems.
_____	7.	Swimming several laps each day is also an excellent exercise for most of the muscle groups.
_____	8.	I exercise by walking a couple of miles every day at a fairly brisk pace.
_____	9.	Recently, people have begun saving many of our old breeds of poultry and livestock.
_____	10.	For a good grade on the final examination, you really should begin reviewing your class notes well in advance.
_____	11.	The old couple supplement their income by raising a flock of turkeys.
_____	12.	Replacing our car's transmission will be quite expensive.
_____	13.	Several books and articles have been written recently on the subject of teaching foreign languages to small children.
_____	14.	Playing a musical instrument requires both determination and persistence.
_____	15.	The boatswain's main job on a ship was overseeing the deck hands.
_____	16.	Michael enjoys collecting stamps from various countries.
_____	17.	By limiting our expenses, we saved an additional $200 a month.
_____	18.	I located some information for my research paper by using the Internet.
_____	19.	Did they finish painting the living room?
_____	20.	Reading literature in its original language will give you a better knowledge of its exact meaning.
_____	21.	The last task of the Bowmans' work day is milking their thirty dairy cows.
_____	22.	Before using any technology you should consider the ramifications of its use.
_____	23.	Neil Postman has written about the dangers of watching television thoughtlessly and uncritically.
_____	24.	Marjorie enjoys making her and her children's clothes.
_____	25.	The Constitution was a means of preventing the inordinate growth of government.

Exercise 27: Gerund Phrases

Underline the verbs twice and the subjects once.
Label all complements (PN, PA, DO, IO, OC, RO).
Put a wavy line under the gerund.
Put parentheses around the gerund phrase.
In the blank at the left tell how the gerund phrase is used by writing S (subject), PN (predicate nominative), DO (direct object), OP (object of a preposition), etc.

_____ 1. Contraditory impulses toward concentration and fragmentation went into the making of our peculiar system of "one and many." —M. E. Bradford

_____ 2. The twelfth amendment to the Constitution outlines procedures for electing the president and vice president.

_____ 3. By warning about the danger of an activist judiciary, John Taylor is very instructive to our own times.

_____ 4. Alexandr Solzhenitsyn angered Soviet officials by openly criticizing the Communist regime.

_____ 5. Getting into debt early in life may cause you problems for many years.

_____ 6. The proper purpose of the criminal justice system is the protection of the innocent by punishing the guilty.

_____ 7. Needless to say, his smoking for thirty years was the cause of his emphysema.

_____ 8. I am quite concerned, Joe, about your missing so many classes recently.

_____ 9. Studying medieval literature can teach us about all aspects of the culture of the period.

_____ 10. Will's primary responsibility is mowing the grass and trimming the hedges.

_____ 11. One of our goals must be helping the poor in our own communities.

_____ 12. Sleeping on guard duty was grounds for a court martial and the death penalty.

_____ 13. We must give our attention to plowing our own fields and tending our own crops.

_____ 14. What will be accomplished by putting off this decision until a later time?

_____ 15. Before starting your research paper, read several short encyclopedia articles on the subject.

_____ 16. Our first task of the day was feeding all the stock.

_____ 17. The young couple enjoyed walking along the beach together.

_____ 18. Socrates was executed for not believing in the gods and for corrupting the youth of Athens.

_____ 19. By rotating the crops we can increase yields significantly

_____ 20. My singing in the shower bothered everyone in the house.

_____ 21. The Agrarians deserve belated tribute for having been premature environmentalists.
       —Eugene Genovese

_____ 22. We were certainly appreciative for our neighbors' helping us after the tornado.

_____ 23. Seeing those constellations will necessitate a higher magnitude telescope.

_____ 24. My sister has always enjoyed acting in amateur theatricals.

_____ 25. I do not understand his speaking in such a cruel way.

Exercise 28: Participial Phrases and Gerund Phrases

Underline the verbs twice and the subjects once.
Label all complements (PN, PA, DO, IO, OC, RO).
Put a wavy line under the verbal.
Put parentheses around the verbal phrase.
In the left blank tell whether the phrase is a participial phrase (PART) or a gerund phrase (GER).
If it is a participial phrase, in the right blank give the noun or pronoun it modifies.
If it is a gerund phrase, in the right blank tell how it is used by writing S (subject), PN (predicate nominative), DO (direct object), OP (object of a preposition), etc.

1. Looking through the telescope, the astronomer examined the rings of Saturn.

2. Who could have predicted the dangers awaiting us on shore?

3. After weighing all the evidence, the jury finally came to a unanimous verdict.

4. Many aquaducts built by the Romans are still standing throughout Europe.

5. In your opinion, what is the first step in conquering any addiction?

6. Among other things, the job of a librarian is providing books and periodicals as support for the academic classes.

7. Four girls singing in the college choir got the flu.

8. The president did not mention meeting with representatives of the major labor unions.

9. Did the person answering the telephone give you any information about the job?

10. One of the secretary's tasks is answering the telephone.

11. In his famous speech, Churchill described Soviet totalitarianism as an iron curtain descending across Europe "from Stettin in the Baltic to Trieste in the Adriatic."

12. They were standing there, gazing into the sky.

13. My brothers enjoy participating in all types of sports.

14. The terrible consequences arising out of this one wrong decision cannot be imagined now.

15. Several poems written by Tennyson concern Arthurian legend.

16. Having overslept once again, I was late for my first-period class.

17. A large banner hanging from an upstairs window welcomed us home.

Exercise 29: Infinitives Used as Adjectives

Underline the verbs twice and the subjects once.
Label all complements (PN, PA, DO, IO, OC, RO).
Put a wavy line under the infinitive.
Put parentheses around the infinitive phrase.
In the blank at the left write the noun or pronoun that the infinitive phrase is modifying.

_____ 1. The devil hath power to assume a pleasing shape. —William Shakespeare

_____ 2. I will defend to the death your right to be wrong.

_____ 3. Camay is the soap to use for smooth skin.

_____ 4. Is this the road to take to Charlottesville?

_____ 5. Dickens's story of the death of Little Nell made people cry on both sides of the Atlantic.

_____ 6. The book to read on Winston Churchill is Manchester's *The Last Lion*.

_____ 7. Is there any evidence to support his assertions?

_____ 8. I have no reason to doubt his veracity.

_____ 9. Do we not have a just cause to fight for?

_____ 10. Is there a way to keep dampness out of the basement?

_____ 11. A close analysis of English sentences is the only successful method to teach English syntax.

_____ 12. Ralph made a motion to table the proposal, and I seconded it.

_____ 13. The soldiers undertook one last attempt to free the captives.

_____ 14. Her efforts to obtain an education were finally crowned with success.

_____ 15. Unfortunately, there were no rivets to repair the hull of the riverboat.

_____ 16. We were surprised by his eagerness to help us.

_____ 17. Documents to verify the ownership of the property were not available.

_____ 18. Before penicillin, there simply were no drugs to cure such infections.

_____ 19. The poem to be memorized by the class is an old English ballad.

_____ 20. The Maya considered the potato the best crop to grow at these high altitudes.

_____ 21. Our father was in no mood to be contradicted.

_____ 22. Is there any way to stop the influx of illegal immigrants?

_____ 23. A society to propogate Christian knowledge throughout the world was established in England in 1698.

_____ 24. The importance of Wesley's efforts to evangelize the people of Britain can hardly be overestimated.

Exercise 30: Infinitives Used as Nouns

Underline the verbs twice and the subjects once.
Label all complements (PN, PA, DO, IO, OC, RO).
Put a wavy line under the infinitive.
Put parentheses around the infinitive phrase.
In the blank at the left tell how the infinitive phrase is used by writing S (subject), PN (predicate nominative), DO (direct object), OP (object of a preposition), etc.

_____ 1. To be brave is not enough. —W. J. Turner

_____ 2. Teach me, my God and King, in all things Thee to see. —George Herbert

_____ 3. In the Declaration of Independence, Jefferson attempted to give the Americans' grievances against Great Britain.

_____ 4. Bunyan's goal was to display the Christian life in an allegory.

_____ 5. Eddie did nothing except sit around all afternoon and watch television.

_____ 6. The objects of Drake's journey were to gain wealth for himself, to gain fame for his nation, and to rout the Spanish.

_____ 7. Scipio ordered Carthage to be completely destroyed.

_____ 8. Mrs. Jones taught me to play the organ.

_____ 9. The old man's desire was to plant trees throughout the barren land.

_____ 10. I did everything except make the beds.

_____ 11. To speak hard truths in a kind way is indeed difficult.

_____ 12. Everyone wanted him to make a speech.

_____ 13. Sam asked Abigail to go with him to the concert.

_____ 14. Did they decide to paint the room yellow?

_____ 15. My suggestion to my wife was to paint all the trim the same color.

_____ 16. During her sisters' false declarations of love for King Lear, Cordelia could do nothing but remain silent.

_____ 17. To get rid of these insidious non-native plant species will be extremely difficult.

_____ 18. It is wrong to laugh at another's weakness.

_____ 19. The goal of these explorers was to find a water route to the Indies.

_____ 20. Was his plan always to go to medical school?

_____ 21. Surely to ignore almost six thousand years of moral and ethical consensus is, at least, unwise.

_____ 22. Why does your physician want you to take more vitamin D?

_____ 23. Robinson Crusoe chose to ignore his father's instruction and become a sailor.

_____ 24. According to Christ, to love God with all the heart, soul, and mind is the greatest commandment.

_____ 25. The second commandment is to love our neighbor.

Exercise 31: Infinitives Used as Adverbs Modifying Verbs

Underline the verbs twice and the subjects once.
Label all complements (PN, PA, DO, IO, OC, RO).
Put a wavy line under the infinitive.
Put parentheses around the infinitive phrase.
In the blank at the left write the verb that the infinitive phrase is modifying.

_____	1.	I come to bury Caesar. —William Shakespeare
_____	2.	To do well on the vocabulary test, you should review a little each day.
_____	3.	The people went to Dover to see the queen.
_____	4.	We left early to avoid the traffic.
_____	5.	After 1741, Handel abandoned opera to dedicate himself to the composition of oratorios.
_____	6.	Our team traveled to Louisville to compete in the basketball tournament there.
_____	7.	After his release from the hospital, Mr. Greaves entered a convalescent home in Birmingham to undergo physical therapy.
_____	8.	To read more about the Agrarians, consult Professor Cowan's book.
_____	9.	The colonists did not remain in the East long; soon, to obtain better land, they had crossed the mountains.
_____	10.	We flew to the runway at the edge of the jungle to deliver some supplies and to drop off two passengers.
_____	11.	I went across the room to get a better look at the painting.
_____	12.	After the outbreak of the war Lee was persuaded to take the command of the Army of Northern Virginia.
_____	13.	The English shepherd dog was bred to drive sheep, cattle, and other livestock.
_____	14.	In 1664 Charles II sent a fleet to seize the Dutch colony of New Amsterdam.
_____	15.	Many people in large cities like New York depend on subways to get them from place to place.
_____	16.	Many Jews moved to America even during the colonial period to escape religious persecution in Europe.
_____	17.	To make a shoo-fly pie you will need molasses, brown sugar, and flour.
_____	18.	My father climbed up to the attic to look for a leak in the roof.
_____	19.	Because of the famine in Canaan, the brothers of Joseph had been sent to Egypt to purchase grain for the family.
_____	20.	To get into graduate school students must maintain a high grade point average and do well on the Graduate Record Examination.

Exercise 32: Infinitives Used as Adverbs Modifying Adjectives

Underline the verbs twice and the subjects once.
Label all complements (PN, PA, DO, IO, OC, RO).
Put a wavy line under the infinitive.
Put parentheses around the infinitive phrase.
In the blank at the left write the adjective that the infinitive phrase is modifying.

_____	1. Miss Anderson will be very glad to answer any of your questions.
_____	2. God is not ashamed to be called their God. —Hebrews 11:16
_____	3. The class seemed quite unprepared to take the examination.
_____	4. I am reluctant to give a scholarship to a student with such a low grade point average.
_____	5. The children were not happy to be going to bed so early.
_____	6. Why weren't they willing to contribute a little of their time?
_____	7. In the current financial climate, the board of trustees did not feel able to give the faculty a larger raise.
_____	8. The Soviets were eager to extend their empire throughout the world.
_____	9. We were unhappy to learn the outcome of the election.
_____	10. Because of a birth defect he is unable to walk without a slight limp.
_____	11. Fallen man is powerless to free himself from bondage to sin.
_____	12. Anxious to hear the results of the race, we crowded around the television.
_____	13. The team, eager to win the championship, practiced harder and longer.
_____	14. Having alienated most of his earlier supporters, he was almost sure to lose the election.
_____	15. Be sure to change the oil every three thousand miles.
_____	16. All of us, of course, were shocked to hear of the tragedy.
_____	17. Five people are prepared to testify about his presence at the time of the murder.
_____	18. Despite their valiant efforts, Belgium and the Netherlands were absolutely impotent to stop the Nazi blitzkrieg in 1940.
_____	19. They hired someone qualified to design the electrical and plumbing system for the factory.
_____	20. Dale was unprepared to answer such detailed questions about the audit.

Exercise 33: Infinitives Used as Adverbs Modifying Adverbs

Underline the verbs twice and the subjects once.
Label all complements (PN, PA, DO, IO, OC, RO).
Put a wavy line under the infinitive.
Put parentheses around the infinitive phrase.
In the blank at the left write the adverb that the infinitive phrase is modifying.

_____	1.	The planets are too far away to be seen with the naked eye.
_____	2.	We talked quietly enough to avoid being overheard.
_____	3.	Melvin is too short to be a highway patrolman.
_____	4.	There are simply too many stars in the sky to be counted.
_____	5.	Is this corn sufficiently ripe to be picked now?
_____	6.	Were your seats close enough to give you a good view of the stage?
_____	7.	Night came too swiftly for us to finish all our chores.
_____	8.	These statistics are too outdated to be relevant in this present argument.
_____	9.	The gymnast's marks were insufficiently good to obtain for her the gold medal.
_____	10.	I am just too tired to go anywhere tonight.
_____	11.	You must read closely enough to get the main idea in each paragraph.
_____	12.	Is pine sufficiently durable to be used for fence posts?
_____	13.	His parents considered him too young to be left alone.
_____	14.	The examinee performed insufficiently well to win a scholarship.
_____	15.	They did not stay long enough to hear the verdict.
_____	16.	My father arrived too late to hear my brother's trombone solo.
_____	17.	This computer's functions are too limited to handle this amount of data.
_____	18.	Evan, are you tall enough to reach those boxes on the top shelf without a ladder?
_____	19.	The rooms of their new house are insufficiently large to hold all the furniture from their old house.
_____	20.	But is he wise enough to recognize his own mistake?
_____	21.	Unfortunately, the language of many great writers, such as Chaucer, or perhaps even Shakespeare, is too archaic to be easily understood by many students.
_____	22.	They must read those authors often enough to become familiar with their vocabulary and diction.
_____	23.	The candidate did not answer the question sufficiently to put the matter to rest.
_____	24.	He was insufficiently prepared to answer our questions.
_____	25.	The cabinet was too small to hold all our books.

Exercise 34: Infinitive Phrases

Underline the verbs twice and the subjects once.
Label all complements (PN, PA, DO, IO, OC, RO).
Put a wavy line under the infinitive.
Put parentheses around the infinitive phrase.
In the left blank, tell whether the phrase is used as an adjective (ADJ), an adverb (ADV), or a noun (N).
If the infinitive phrase is used as an adjective, in the right blank give the noun or pronoun it is modifying.
If the infinitive phrase is used as an adverb, in the right blank give the verb, adjective, or adverb it is modifying.
If the infinitive phrase is used as a noun, in the right blank tell how it is used by writing S (subject), PN (predicate nominative), DO (direct object), OP (object of a preposition), etc.

1. To tell lies about someone—deliberately and maliciously—is almost unpardonable.
2. Each of us has his own job to do.
3. To play the piano well, you must practice every day.
4. Columbus's intention, of course, was to sail west to the Indies.
5. We must come up with some way to avoid this type of situation in the future.
6. About halfway through our hike it began to rain.
7. In your opinion, why is a principled politician so difficult to find these days?
8. Most stars are too far away to be seen with the naked eye.
9. With such a cynical attitude, he was certain to be unhappy.
10. She did nothing except raise her voice louder and louder.
11. The defendant had nothing to say in response to the charges.
12. The Discipline Committee is now ready to see you.
13. Unfortunately, Poland was not powerful enough to resist the Nazi blitzkrieg.
14. To provide for our families in case of our untimely deaths, most of us purchase life insurance.
15. In his delightful *Chronicles of Narnia*, C. S. Lewis attempts to retell the Christian story of redemption in the form of a fantasy.
16. The violinist was asked to play yet another song.
17. Diana's goal was to become a pediatrician.
18. To measure the amount of radiation, scientists use a seismograph.
19. Why did he want to drop that class?
20. He did not have sufficient time to study for all his classes.
21. Steve has always wanted to play on a professional baseball team.
22. They were unwilling to cede that point to their opponents.
23. According to one poet, it takes "a heap of living to make a house a home."
24. Is this the piano to be tuned?
25. They seemed genuinely sorry to hear of our misfortune.

Exercise 35: Infinitive Phrases

Underline the verbs twice and the subjects once.
Label all complements (PN, PA, DO, IO, OC, RO).
Put a wavy line under the infinitive.
Put parentheses around the infinitive phrase.
In the left blank, tell whether the phrase is used as an adjective (ADJ), an adverb (ADV), or a noun (N).
If the infinitive phrase is used as an adjective, in the right blank give the noun or pronoun it is modifying.
If the infinitive phrase is used as an adverb, in the right blank give the verb, adjective, or adverb it is modifying.
If the infinitive phrase is used as a noun, in the right blank tell how it is used by writing S (subject), PN (predicate nominative), DO (direct object), OP (object of a preposition), etc.

1. To err is human. —Alexander Pope

2. What is the best book to consult for information on quasars?

3. To master the Latin language, you must give a great deal of attention to the various verb forms.

4. Buckminster Fuller attempted to construct a geodesic dome of lightweight materials.

5. She took the children to the mall to purchase school clothes.

6. The library staff will be glad to assist you in your bibliographic research.

7. At the very least, the goal of Patrick Henry and the other Anti-Federalists was to obtain a clear constitutional statement of the rights of individual citizens and the states.

8. Is this the road to take to Chincoteague?

9. Have you read far enough in *Othello* to discover the real motives of Iago?

10. I was urged by my parents to think seriously about my decision.

11. Professor Dawkins was sure to be upset at our poor performance on the mid-term examination.

12. Paul went to Mars Hill to confront the Athenian philosophers.

13. Before the storm the boys had done everything except trim the hedge.

14. Churchill urged the people of Great Britain to prepare for an invasion by the Germans.

15. I have come to pay my bill.

16. Balsa is the wood to use for model airplanes.

17. To understand the text completely requires a knowledge of the original language.

18. The pioneers traveled farther to the north to avoid barren deserts farther south.

19. That is not the correct pronoun to use in that sentence.

20. We went to Amsterdam primarily to visit the famous Rijk Museum.

21. The children have been wanting to go to the fair for some time.

22. Quinine is the medicine to take for malaria.

Exercise 36: Verbal Phrases

Underline the verbs twice and the subjects once.
Label all complements (PN, PA, DO, IO, OC, RO).
Put a wavy line under the verbal.
Put parentheses around the verbal phrase.
In the left blank, tell whether the verbal phrase is a participle (PART), gerund (GER), or infinitive (INF).
If the verbal phrase is used as an adjective, in the right blank give the noun or pronoun it is modifying.
If the verbal phrase is used as an adverb, in the right blank give the verb, adjective, or adverb it is modifying.
If the verbal phrase is used as a noun, in the right blank tell how it is used by writing S (subject), PN (predicate nominative),
DO (direct object), OP (object of a preposition), etc.

_____ _____ 1. At the Constitutional Convention, the framers decided to scrap the Articles of Confederation and to write a new constitution.

_____ _____ 2. As a result of one compromise reached at the Convention, Congress has two houses, the Senate and the House of Representatives.

_____ _____ 3. The House is composed of representatives chosen on the basis of the population of the states.

_____ _____ 4. Having two senators from each state guarantees equality of both small and large states in the Senate.

_____ _____ 5. Senators, originally elected by the state legislatures, represented the interests of the various states.

_____ _____ 6. You can begin a career in politics by participating in local activities like school boards and county commissions.

_____ _____ 7. Recently, I have enjoyed reading the new biography of Thomas Jefferson.

_____ _____ 8. To protect the rights of individual persons and the states, they added the Bill of Rights to the Constitution.

_____ _____ 9. Are mere political interests strong enough to unite a nation?

_____ _____ 10. Are not religion and morality necessary to support the habits of republican government?

_____ _____ 11. The basis of our political systems is the right of the people to make and to alter their constitutions of government. —George Washington

_____ _____ 12. Having served two terms, Washington wisely declined a third.

_____ _____ 13. Bills passed in one house of Congress must be approved by the other house as well.

_____ _____ 14. The role of the president is to preserve, protect, and defend the Constitution of the United States.

_____ _____ 15. My favorite part of our tour of Washington was visiting the Supreme Court.

_____ _____ 16. To defend us from ourselves, we have a set of checks and balances in our government.

_____ _____ 17. The power to declare war is given to Congress.

Exercise 37: Verbal Phrases

Underline the verbs twice and the subjects once.
Label all complements (PN, PA, DO, IO, OC, RO).
Put a wavy line under the verbal.
Put parentheses around the verbal phrase.
In the left blank, tell whether the verbal phrase is a participle (PART), gerund (GER), or infinitive (INF).
If the verbal phrase is used as an adjective, in the right blank give the noun or pronoun it is modifying.
If the verbal phrase is used as an adverb, in the right blank give the verb, adjective, or adverb it is modifying.
If the verbal phrase is used as a noun, in the right blank tell how it is used by writing S (subject), PN (predicate nominative), DO (direct object), OP (object of a preposition), etc.

_____ _____   1.   The Indo-European family includes langauges spoken from western China to the Atlantic.

_____ _____   2.   Sir William Jones was the first to discover the connections between Sanskrit and the classical languages of Europe.

_____ _____   3.   Learning a foreign language requires a thorough knowledge of the vocabulary and the grammar.

_____ _____   4.   The New Testament is written in the common dialect used in the Hellenic world.

_____ _____   5.   The Romans, having conquered Italy, extended their empire throughout much of the Western world.

_____ _____   6.   To read the great Roman authors, you must study Latin.

_____ _____   7.   King Alfred wanted to obtain translations of the Bible and other books.

_____ _____   8.   The Romany, also called Gypsies, originated in India.

_____ _____   9.   Aunt Clara's favorite pastime is doing crossword puzzles.

_____ _____   10.   By examining the cuneiform tablets, scholars have discovered much about the Babylonians.

_____ _____   11.   The Germanic tribes invading Britain in the fifth century introduced Old English to the island.

_____ _____   12.   Our professor wanted us to read *The Canterbury Tales* in their original Middle English.

_____ _____   13.   In Ireland, Scotland, Wales, and Britanny you can still find people speaking the Celtic languages.

_____ _____   14.   Is it possible to have national unity without a common language?

_____ _____   15.   Our regional and ethnic varieties of English, reaching back to the original settlement of our country, remind us of our past and connect us with our families.

_____ _____   16.   Shakespeare had one of the largest vocabularies of any writer living at that time.

_____ _____   17.   Many words derived from Latin and Greek sources entered the English language at the time of the Renaissance.

Exercise 38: Appositives

Underline the verbs twice and the subjects once.
Label all complements (PN, PA, DO, IO, OC, RO).
Put parentheses around each appositive phrase.
Draw an arrow to the noun or pronoun that the appositive phrase is renaming.

1. My brother Daniel recently completed his hospital residency and established his own medical practice.

2. *The Spirit of St. Louis*, Charles Lindbergh's famous airplane, can now be seen in the Smithsonian.

3. Are you familiar with T. S. Eliot, the twentieth-century poet and critic?

4. There is a huge difference in thought and technique between *The Wasteland*, his major early work, and his later poems.

5. The science fiction of the French writer Jules Verne was amazingly prescient.

6. Williamsburg, the colonial capital of Virginia, has been restored to its eighteenth-century appearance.

7. The origin of the Jewish holiday Hanukkah can be found in the apocryphal books of the Maccabees.

8. In *To Kill a Mockingbird*, Harper Lee's first novel, we see a classic depiction of the clash of loyalties.

9. That college is named for Ann Judson, the first female American foreign missionary.

10. The French aristocrat the Marquis de Lafayette came to America to help the struggling colonies in their revolution against tyranny.

11. Sorghum, a source of delicious syrup, can be grown under a large variety of soil and weather conditions.

12. "The people of the book" is the term for Jews and Christians in the Koran, the sacred text of Islam.

13. The sphygmomanometer, an instrument with a rubber bulb and a numerical gauge, is used to measure arterial blood pressure.

14. The Lawn, the oldest part of the University of Virginia, contains the original buildings of "Mr. Jefferson's university."

15. The modern college quadrangle has its origins in the cloister, the garden and structures at the center of a medieval monastery.

16. Ironically, the Nobel Peace Prize was funded by Alfred Nobel, the famous inventor of dynamite.

17. The Soviet Union was built on communism, a system of thought at odds with both physical and spiritual realities.

18. His dissertation is a lengthy discussion of the Greek word *baptizo* and its many uses in classical and Biblical literature.

19. The works of Southern writer Flannery O'Connor are suffused with a concern for spiritual values.

20. Much of recent art is a product of post-modernism, a philosophy without moral or rational absolutes.

21. The winner of the speech contest was my cousin Meg.

22. Guinevere, King Arthur's queen, was unfaithful to him.

23. Free Will Baptist missionary Laura Belle Barnard worked with the "untouchables" of South India.

24. We visited Westminster Abbey, the burial place of many famous Britons.

Exercise 39: Appositives

Underline the verbs twice and the subjects once.
Label all complements (PN, PA, DO, IO, OC, RO).
Put parentheses around each appositive phrase.
Draw an arrow to the noun or pronoun that the appositive phrase is renaming.

1. Labor to keep alive in your breast that little spark of celestial fire, conscience. —George Washington

2. He received some assistance with his college expenses from his brother, a successful lawyer in Cincinatti.

3. In the sixth month the angel Gabriel was sent from God unto a city of Galilee named Nazareth. —Luke 1:26

4. His dream, to have a little farm of his own, seemed quite unobtainable.

5. The vast majority of inhabitants of the South from the Revolution to the Civil War can best be described by the term *yeomen*.

6. Most of our knowledge of the life of Samuel Johnson comes from Boswell, his friend and biographer.

7. He was engaged in his favorite pastime, napping.

8. The history of the two ancient British universities, Oxford and Cambridge, is marked by many scholars and a few fools.

9. Luke, the beloved physician, and Demas greet you. —Colossians 4:14

10. Henry VIII's second wife, Anne Boleyn, was the mother of Elizabeth I.

11. At the drop of a hat, or with even less incentive, Alice's father will recite his favorite poem, "The Cremation of Sam McGee."

12. Many Scots celebrate the birthday of Robert Burns, their national poet.

13. The early English play *Everyman* gives a clear presentation of medieval Roman Catholic theology.

14. The well-loved old ballad "Barbara Allen," though having disappeared from its native home in Britain, survived in many versions throughout the Southern Backcountry of America.

15. One of the most common surgeries is the appendectomy, the removal of the appendix.

16. My cousin Gator obtained his nickname by hatching some alligator eggs next to the kitchen stove.

17. Our candidate is a child of Virginia, "the mother of Presidents."

18. My brethren, have not the faith of our Lord Jesus Christ, the Lord of Glory, with respect of persons. —James 2:1

19. The girl's lovely apparel included a cap and apron of white organdy, a thin, almost transparent muslin.

20. Do you know Mr. Breen, the owner of the department store downtown?

21. He introduced me to his fiancée, Cindy Bowman, and invited me to the wedding.

22. Pizarro, the Spanish conqueror of Peru, cruelly defeated and enslaved the Incas.

23. My favorite character in *David Copperfield* is Betsy Trotwood, David's aunt.

24. Both Paul and his companion Silas were imprisoned in Philippi.

25. Nathan Hawkins, an alumnus and a substantial contributor, received a presidential award.

Exercise 40: Nominatives Absolute

Underline the verbs twice and the subjects once.
Label all complements (PN, PA, DO, IO, OC, RO).
Put a wavy line under the participle.
Put parentheses around the nominative absolute phrase.

1. The rain having stopped, we decided to go ahead with the picnic.

2. I being opposed to the idea, they did not pursue it further.

3. All the offices are closed, today being the Fourth of July.

4. The cashier's office having closed already, I could not cash my check.

5. The horse plunged down the track, the poor jockey holding on for dear life.

6. His little daughter stood there penitently, her eyes red from crying.

7. It was a good holiday, all things considered.

8. Weather permitting, the ceremony will be held in the Rose Garden of the White House.

9. We began somewhat late, our committee chairman having been stuck in traffic.

10. He being aware of the situation, I asked his advice about the matter.

11. Her head full of plans for the holidays, Sarah could not concentrate on her final examination.

12. The night was pitch-black, the moon being obscured by heavy clouds.

13. She being extremely shy, I volunteered to go with her to the dean's office.

14. My radiator having sprung a leak, my engine soon overheated.

15. It being late already, we decided to postpone our trip to the next day.

16. Their first attempt having failed, they resolved to try again.

17. The sun having set, the temperature plummeted.

18. My polite requests and regular memoranda having done no good, I pursued a less pacific approach.

19. We were able to come home with Donald, he having been kind enough to give us a ride.

20. The azaleas being in full bloom, I took several photographs of the house and gardens.

21. The magi having come to Jerusalem, they sought an audience with Herod.

22. We have postponed the planting, the ground being too wet.

23. The winds having reached seventy-five miles an hour, the tropical storm was now a hurricane.

24. The sky growing steadily darker and the winds blowing harder, we retreated to the interior of the house to wait out the storm.

25. My algebra homework being finished, I lay down for a brief nap.

Exercise 41: Phrases

In the blank at the left, identify each italicized phrase by writing PART (participial phrase), GER (gerund phrase), INF (infinitive phrase), APP (appositive phrase), or NOM ABS (nominative absolute phrase).

_____ 1. Gold was discovered at Sutter's Mill in 1849 by men *working at a sawmill.*

_____ 2. Many people from around the country traveled to California *to search for gold.*

_____ 3. *The day being quite hot,* the livestock were lying in the shade of the trees.

_____ 4. Mrs. Bedsole, *a professional genealogist,* will research your family and provide you with detailed information about your ancestors.

_____ 5. Having dug the beds thoroughly, we were now ready *to plant the various perennials.*

_____ 6. Doug entertained the crowd by *playing old tunes on the fiddle.*

_____ 7. A large company of soldiers *hidden in the woods* were preparing an attack on the enemy camp.

_____ 8. *Making fine wooden furniture* requires a thorough knowledge of the tools of the trade.

_____ 9. The Spanish explorer *Ferdinand Magellan* did not complete the circumnavigation of the globe, but his compatriots did.

_____ 10. Are these the best sources *to consult for information on the tribespeople of the Ivory Coast?*

_____ 11. The moss *hanging from the trees* is actually not a parasite really.

_____ 12. It is not a parasite but an epiphyte, *obtaining its nutrients and moisture from the air and rain.*

_____ 13. *To reduce the cost of the new house,* we limited the over-all square footage.

_____ 14. A new house *recently built just down the street* is now the largest house in the neighborhood.

_____ 15. At Christmas break I rode with Darlene as far as St. Louis, *she having offered me a ride with her and her sister.*

_____ 16. At the book sale *held by the college library* I purchased a dictionary and several novels.

_____ 17. The goal of the mission was *to land a man on the moon and return him safely to earth.*

_____ 18. Miss Callaway recommended several articles by Richard Greaves, *the eminent scholar on seventeenth-century Dissenters.*

_____ 19. We explored several poems *written in different poetic meters.*

_____ 20. *The letter having been written by an eyewitness,* it is a major source of evidence about that famous volcanic eruption.

_____ 21. In my opinion, it is too late *to start now.*

_____ 22. My mother gives a great deal of time to *working in her flower garden.*

_____ 23. You can conserve moisture in the ground by *putting down a heavy layer of mulch.*

_____ 24. *Being a class officer* brings with it certain responsibilities.

_____ 25. We certainly appreciate *your helping us in this matter.*

English Grammar and Composition Workbook

Exercise 42: Phrases

Underline the verbs twice and the subjects once.
Label all complements (PN, PA, DO, IO, OC, RO).
Put wavy lines under all verbals.
Put parentheses around all verbal phrases, appositives, and nominatives absolute.
In the left blank, tell whether the phrase is a participial phrase (PART), a gerund phrase (GER), an infinitive phrase (INF), an appositive (APP), or a nominative absolute (NOM ABS).
If the phrase is used as an adjective, in the right blank give the noun or pronoun it is modifying.
If the phrase is used as an adverb, in the right blank give the verb, adjective, or adverb it is modifying.
If the phrase is used as a noun, in the right blank tell how it is used by writing S (subject), PN (predicate nominative), DO (direct object), OP (object of a preposition), etc.
If the phrase is an appositive, in the right blank give the noun or pronoun it is renaming.
If the phrase is a nominative absolute, leave the right blank empty.

_____ _____ 1. The nurse came into the room to take my blood pressure and temperature.

_____ _____ 2. Singing these operatic arias by Puccini will require a good knowledge of Italian pronunciation.

_____ _____ 3. The scientists were studying the various life forms living in the hot volcanic pools.

_____ _____ 4. Michael Behe, a prominent writer on the idea of intelligent design, has repeatedly shown the scientific inadequacies of Darwinism.

_____ _____ 5. For instance, what is the statistical possibility of the human eye's having developed by means of evolution?

_____ _____ 6. The hurricane having taken a northerly direction, the people along the Florida panhandle prepared for the worst.

_____ _____ 7. Upon graduation, Gerald planned to attend medical school in Baltimore.

_____ _____ 8. To write correctly and effectively, one must have a good grasp of English grammar and usage first.

_____ _____ 9. Meteorologists now use satellite photography to predict the weather.

_____ _____ 10. Is this the road to take to Valdosta?

_____ _____ 11. My sister Martha and her husband live on a farm in northern Mississippi.

_____ _____ 12. The words inscribed on the outside of the box have confounded most archaeologists.

_____ _____ 13. We certainly appreciate your helping us out in this matter.

_____ _____ 14. Right up to its ultimate demise, the Soviet Union was determined to extend its evil empire by means of military power.

_____ _____ 15. Surely every people deserves the right to determine its own government and political structures.

_____ _____ 16. We put up the bluebird houses built by the boys.

_____ _____ 17. A schedule listing all the various courses of the college and their times and locations is published each semester and made available for all potential students.

_____ _____ 18. Severe destruction was caused in the area by tornadoes spun off by the hurricane.

_____ _____ 19. The president's hope is to reduce the complexity of the current federal tax code.

_____ _____ 20. Is this computer powerful enough to handle such a huge amount of statistical data?

_____ _____ 21. The electricity having gone out, we lit several candles and placed them on the table.

_____ _____ 22. The concept of the just war developed by Thomas Aquinas takes into consideration both the need for human justice and the real negative results of human revenge.

_____ _____ 23. Eileen enjoys participating in amateur theatricals.

_____ _____ 24. The bridge spanning Lawson Creek was washed out in the flood.

_____ _____ 25. The English poet Robert Herrick wrote various poems about rural customs in seventeenth-century Devon.

_____ _____ 26. Stalactites and stalagmites are formed by water dripping from the ceiling of a cave.

_____ _____ 27. The limestone dissolved in the water accumulates and forms those rocky structures on the roof or floor of the cave.

_____ _____ 28. Joey wanted to visit Mammoth Cave during our trip to Kentucky.

_____ _____ 29. The title of Chinua Achebe's novel, taken from the poetry of Yeats, carries a sinister connotation.

_____ _____ 30. After removing the old shingles, we piled them in the back of the truck.

_____ _____ 31. Sir Winston Churchill asked Americans to come to the aid of Great Britain.

_____ _____ 32. To produce a mighty book you must choose a mighty theme. —Herman Melville

_____ _____ 33. The stock boys did everything except put the boxes away.

_____ _____ 34. A monument dedicated to the memory of the Confederate dead is located in Lee Square dowtown.

_____ _____ 35. Our Revolutionary War ancestors resisted the attempts of the British king and Parliament to rob us of our rights as Englishmen.

_____ _____ 36. Canadian geese flying south for the winter can frequently be seen in the late autumn sky.

_____ _____ 37. Some of the American troops in the Revolution were commanded by Casimir Pulaski, a Polish general.

_____ _____ 38. The night being cold, we retreated indoors.

_____ _____ 39. The country now called the Czech Republic was once known as Bohemia.

_____ _____ 40. We found several umbrellas left in the rack by the front door.

_____ _____ 41. Early English poetry, though written in an alliterative pattern, had no formal meter or rhyme scheme.

_____ _____ 42. The green truck parked at the end is mine.

English Grammar and Composition Workbook

Exercise 43: Adjective Clauses

Underline the verbs twice and the subjects once.
Label all complements (PN, PA, DO, IO, OC, RO).
Put brackets around the adjective clause.
In the blank at the left, give the noun or pronoun that the adjective clause is modifying.

                1.   The family who live in that house are cousins of ours.

                2.   Give these folders to the people whose names are on them.

                3.   The girl whom Frank married grew up near my home in Virginia.

                4.   The sea which stretched before the Jews seemed an insurmountable barrier for them.

                5.   Were you familiar with the piece by Chopin that Deborah played?

                6.   Yorktown was the place where the Revolution, for all practical purposes, came to an end.

                7.   They moved here in 1986, when Kathy was in third grade.

                8.   Do you know the name of the person with whom he spoke?

                9.   A Geiger counter is an instrument by which the level of radioactivity can be measured.

              10.   Did they discover the reason why the electricity was off?

              11.   Queen Charlotte, wife of King George III, is the one for whom the city of Charlotte, North Carolina is named.

              12.   Wasn't Fleming the one who discovered penicillin?

              13.   What did you do with the package that I put on the counter?

              14.   The person whom I wrote the letter to is the vice-president of the corporation.

              15.   The pandas we saw at the zoo in Washington are on loan from China.

              16.   I have no respect for a person who will not pay his honest debts.

              17.   The one to whom we entrusted our safety turned out to be untrustworthy.

              18.   The new drapes which she hung up in the living room are made of blue cotton damask.

              19.   Is there a convenient time when we can meet for a discussion of this situation?

              20.   The Cumberland Gap was a spot where settlers could more easily cross the Appalachian Mountains.

              21.   The one who wrote the play was Ben Jonson.

              22.   We visited the village in Bavaria where my wife's family had emigrated from.

              23.   The entire concept of "public relations" is one which evolved in the twentieth century along with the mass media.

              24.   One material which was formerly widely used is pewter, a mixture of tin and other metals.

              25.   The man to whom those sonnets were dedicated by Shakespeare has never been absolutely identified.

Exercise 44: Adjective Clauses

Underline the verbs twice and the subjects once.
Label all complements (PN, PA, DO, IO, OC, RO).
Put brackets around the adjective clause.
In the blank at the left, give the noun or pronoun that the adjective clause is modifying.

_____ 1. People who live in glass houses should not throw stones.

_____ 2. He that repeateth a matter separateth very friends. —Proverbs 17:9

_____ 3. There was a time when buffalo could be found practically everywhere in North America.

_____ 4. They built the fort at a place where two rivers met.

_____ 5. A man that hath friends must show himself friendly. —Proverbs 18:24

_____ 6. The modern chain store, which has spread its tentacles throughout the nation, has practically destroyed the small-town store.

_____ 7. The destination of the English General Baptists was Carolina, which offered religious dissenters a haven of sorts.

_____ 8. He that giveth unto the poor shall not lack. —Proverbs 28:27

_____ 9. I did not know the man that spoke to us.

_____ 10. The book I cited the most in my speech is a recent work on the subject of DNA testing.

_____ 11. The name of Queen Victoria, who ruled from 1837 to 1901, has been given to the entire period.

_____ 12. I couldn't find the receipt that I had put in the desk drawer.

_____ 13. He gave himself assiduously to the task which lay in front of him, and he completed it.

_____ 14. Is that the region of China where Western influence was most felt in the nineteenth century?

_____ 15. There's a divinity that shapes our ends. —William Shakespeare

_____ 16. He that steals an egg will steal an ox. —George Herbert

_____ 17. I handed the baton to the next runner, whose hand was outstretched to me.

_____ 18. We entered the small cabin which the settlers had constructed of hewn logs.

_____ 19. In the pasture where the livestock were grazing grew all sorts of lush native grasses.

_____ 20. The companions with whom he was traveling asked him several questions about his family and his occupation.

_____ 21. They discovered several manuscripts which dated back to the tenth century.

_____ 22. Not all who wander are lost. —J. R. R. Tolkien

_____ 23. She is the one for whom he bought the gift.

_____ 24. Are these the clothes which you are donating to Goodwill?

_____ 25. The people from whom we purchased this house moved to Alaska.

Exercise 45: Noun Clauses

Underline the verbs twice and the subjects once.
Label all complements (PN, PA, DO, IO, OC, RO).
Put brackets around the noun clause.
In the blank at the left, tell how the noun clause is used by writing S (subject), PN (predicate nominative), DO (direct object), OP (object of a preposition), etc.

_____ 1. The topic of the meeting was what should be done about the large number of burglaries.

_____ 2. I thought that I had left my boots in the hall closet.

_____ 3. Who steals my purse steals trash. —William Shakespeare

_____ 4. Do you know whose woods these are?

_____ 5. Our teacher told us which textbooks we should purchase.

_____ 6. Do you know where he keeps his hammer?

_____ 7. Whoever gossips to you will also gossip about you.

_____ 8. After a thorough investigation, the police discovered what had happened on the night of the murder.

_____ 9. Tell the jury where you were on the morning of July 15.

_____ 10. Hand these packages to whoever is sitting at the reception desk.

_____ 11. His physician's major concern is that his temperature not rise any further.

_____ 12. His early experiences certainly made him what he is today.

_____ 13. In her best French, she asked him what his name was.

_____ 14. Unfortunately, we were not told what we should do in this situation.

_____ 15. They handed the newspapers to whoever wanted them.

_____ 16. The fact that he is an excellent speaker will certainly help him in politics.

_____ 17. We do not believe that government is our salvation.

_____ 18. His assertion that he was not even in town at the time of the murder seems plausible to me.

_____ 19. She asked Dr. Deel whether the economics class would be offered next semester.

_____ 20. I think it will rain either today or tomorrow.

_____ 21. The passengers were informed that the plane would soon be landing in Dallas.

_____ 22. The judges announced who had won the essay contest.

_____ 23. They naively believed that the formation of an international body would prevent future war.

_____ 24. Where the house should be built must be our first consideration.

_____ 25. I cannot accept the idea that there are not other viable candidates for that office.

Exercise 46: Noun Clauses

Underline the verbs twice and the subjects once.
Label all complements (PN, PA, DO, IO, OC, RO).
Put brackets around the noun clause.
In the blank at the left, tell how the noun clause is used by writing S (subject), PN (predicate nominative), DO (direct object), OP (object of a preposition), etc.

_____ 1. Have the authorities discovered who took the money?

_____ 2. The question on the floor is whether we should raise taxes or not.

_____ 3. That something must be done is now clear to all of us.

_____ 4. Do you know who wrote *The Great Gatsby*?

_____ 5. Whosoever shall call upon the name of the Lord shall be saved. —Acts 2:21

_____ 6. Some people believe nothing except what can be proven by scientific methods.

_____ 7. Many said that it couldn't be done.

_____ 8. Whoso mocketh the poor reproacheth his Maker. —Proverbs 17:5

_____ 9. Who bravely dares must sometimes risk a fall. —Tobias Smollett

_____ 10. We often despise what is most useful to us. —Aesop

_____ 11. Originality and initiative are what I ask for my country. —Robert Frost

_____ 12. The cornerstone of the Christian faith is that God is incarnate in Jesus Christ.

_____ 13. Scholars do not agree about who wrote the Epistle to the Hebrews.

_____ 14. A return to sound fiscal policies is what is needed in our country now.

_____ 15. England expects every man will do his duty. —Lord Nelson

_____ 16. The suggestion that the senior class purchase new curtains for the stage was well received.

_____ 17. Alice showed her sister how she had made the slipcovers.

_____ 18. Whoever has made a voyage up the Hudson must remember the Kaatskill Mountains.

        —Washington Irving

_____ 19. The first-round draft choice will go to whichever team had the worst record last year.

_____ 20. In a few minutes the storm destroyed what had been built over twenty years.

_____ 21. The Lord is my helper; I will not fear what man shall do unto me. —Hebrews 13:6

_____ 22. Reflect on what you read, paragraph by paragraph. —Samuel Taylor Coleridge

_____ 23. The food baskets will be given to whoever truly needs them.

_____ 24. King Josiah knew that Israel had strayed far from the Law of God.

_____ 25. Our class was discussing what Melville meant by the "handsome young sailor" in *Billy Budd*.

Exercise 47: Adjective Clauses and Noun Clauses

Underline the verbs twice and the subjects once.
Label all complements (PN, PA, DO, IO, OC, RO).
Put brackets around the dependent clauses.
In the left blank, tell whether the dependent clause is an adjective clause (ADJ) or a noun clause (N).
If the dependent clause is used as an adjective, in the right blank give the noun or pronoun it is modifying.
If the dependent clause is used as a noun, in the right blank tell how it is used by writing S (subject), PN (predicate nominative), DO (direct object), OP (object of a preposition), etc.

_____ _____ 1. The governor's last point was that our state is in great need of infrastructure improvement.

_____ _____ 2. All of the individuals whom the pollster questioned were against the proposal.

_____ _____ 3. Happiness usually eludes those who seek for it alone.

_____ _____ 4. As a clerk in this store you must respond courteously to whatever the customer says.

_____ _____ 5. The graduate whose composition won the contest was a history major.

_____ _____ 6. We can learn some things about Shakespeare's life from what we read in his plays and poems.

_____ _____ 7. The man for whom you should vote should be well qualified for the job.

_____ _____ 8. The ones with whom you associate color your thinking.

_____ _____ 9. Whoso findeth a wife findeth a good thing. —Proverbs 18:22

_____ _____ 10. I call what he has done a great treachery and treason!

_____ _____ 11. He that loveth pleasure shall be a poor man. —Proverbs 21:17

_____ _____ 12. Pluto is a planet about which scientists have learned very little.

_____ _____ 13. The prosperity which Joseph eventually experienced came only after years of affliction.

_____ _____ 14. The astronomer did not know when the comet would return.

_____ _____ 15. I finally realized that my brother was quite ill.

_____ _____ 16. Those that seek me early shall find me. —Proverbs 8:17

_____ _____ 17. He that lies with dogs riseth with fleas. —George Herbert

_____ _____ 18. William Harvey first described how the blood circulates through the body.

_____ _____ 19. I hope that we have something good for supper.

_____ _____ 20. Do you know what the algebra assignment is?

_____ _____ 21. The first settlement the English made in North America was at Roanoke.

_____ _____ 22. The film which we watched was based on the life of Corrie ten Boom.

_____ _____ 23. Tell me what the temperature is.

_____ _____ 24. This book describes how the medieval cathedrals were built.

_____ _____ 25. The Allied troops blew up the bridge which crossed that river.

Exercise 48: Adjective Clauses and Noun Clauses

Underline the verbs twice and the subjects once.
Label all complements (PN, PA, DO, IO, OC, RO).
Put brackets around the dependent clause.
In the left blank, tell whether the dependent clause is an adjective clause (ADJ) or a noun clause (N).
If the dependent clause is used as an adjective, in the right blank give the noun or pronoun it is modifying.
If the dependent clause is used as a noun, in the right blank tell how it is used by writing S (subject), PN (predicate nominative), DO (direct object), OP (object of a preposition), etc.

1. There was never yet philosopher that could endure the toothache patiently.
    —William Shakespeare

2. The self-same sun that shines upon his court hides not his visage from our cottage. —William Shakespeare

3. Remove not the ancient landmark which thy fathers have set. —Proverbs 22:28

4. Everything you read affects you in some way.

5. Israel's decision that an invasion of Canaan would be too dangerous proved a disastrous decision in the history of the nation.

6. The scholars whom I consulted consider Horace a major Latin poet.

7. Have they yet discovered what the atmosphere of Venus is composed of?

8. The house where Washington was born was unfortunately destroyed long ago.

9. The subject of his brief talk was what should be done in case of a fire.

10. Many of the Huguenots, whom the French forced out of their country, fled to the American colonies.

11. Whom the Lord loveth He chasteneth. —Hebrews 12:6

12. The harpsichord was an earlier instrument from which the piano later was developed.

13. Bogs in which peat is located can be found throughout Ireland.

14. I don't know who purchased the brick house on the corner.

15. Do not give your money or your affections to whoever wants them.

16. The time for complaints about grades which were given last year has already passed.

17. One unusual thing about English is that it contains words from many different languages.

18. The lady who telephoned this morning requested information about the upcoming performance.

19. Do you know who won the World Series?

20. Thomas Grantham, who taught himself several languages, was an amazing scholar.

21. The dean told me that someone's car was being towed.

22. I don't remember what my exact words were.

23. Authorities discovered several people who were planning various acts of terrorism.

Exercise 49: Adverb Clauses

Underline the verbs twice and the subjects once.
Label all complements (PN, PA, DO, IO, OC, RO).
Put brackets around the adverb clause.
In the blank at the left, give the verb, adjective, or adverb the adverb clause is modifying.

_____ 1. The river rose more rapidly than we had expected.

_____ 2. I am happy that you were elected chairman, Denise.

_____ 3. When a thief is hanged, this is not for his own amendment but for the sake of others.
—Thomas Aquinas

_____ 4. Dave can run faster than any other man on the track team.

_____ 5. Rich gifts wax poor when givers prove unkind. —William Shakespeare

_____ 6. Don't fire until you see the whites of their eyes. —Israel Putnam

_____ 7. Even a fool, when he holdeth his peace, is counted wise. —Proverbs 17:28

_____ 8. As soon as Spartan boys were seven years old, they were enrolled in the military.

_____ 9. After the Romans evicted King Tarquin, they set up a republic.

_____ 10. English has changed so significantly over the years that Old English looks like a foreign language.

_____ 11. If chance ruled the world, science would not be possible.

_____ 12. My heart leaps up when I behold a rainbow in the sky. —William Wordsworth

_____ 13. Although we are tired, we must go on.

_____ 14. Yes, Hugh is older than his sister.

_____ 15. I arrived while he was at the library.

_____ 16. I will sing unto the Lord as long as I live. —Psalm 104:33

_____ 17. If you always live with the lame, you will soon limp.

_____ 18. I was curious whether a decision had been reached or not.

_____ 19. Scott can swim better than I.

_____ 20. Because I could not stop for Death, he kindly stopped for me. —Emily Dickinson

_____ 21. As the governor entered the room, everyone stood up.

_____ 22. Are you certain that your request will be granted?

_____ 23. We can meet when you have time.

_____ 24. The travelers waited until the heat of the day was past.

_____ 25. Is Canada larger than the United States in land mass?

Exercise 50: Adverb Clauses

Underline the verbs twice and the subjects once.
Label all complements (PN, PA, DO, IO, OC, RO).
Put brackets around the adverb clause.
In the blank at the left, give the verb, adjective, or adverb the adverb clause is modifying.

_____ 1. I have been in such a pickle since I saw you last. —William Shakespeare

_____ 2. If the world goes against truth, then Athanasius goes against the world. —Athanasius

_____ 3. My days are swifter than a weaver's shuttle. —Job 7:6

_____ 4. As the hart panteth after the water brooks, so panteth my soul after Thee, O God.
—Psalm 42:1

_____ 5. She seems confident that she will be chosen for that role.

_____ 6. There were no major civilizations in Europe until the Minoans established themselves in the Aegean.

_____ 7. Where thou lodgest, I will lodge. —Ruth 1:16

_____ 8. It is snowing harder now than it did this morning.

_____ 9. He died that we might live.

_____ 10. Talk quietly lest you wake the baby.

_____ 11. Saturn was the king of the Titans until his son Jupiter overthrew him.

_____ 12. A man's life is always more forcible than his speech. —Charles Spurgeon

_____ 13. We will leave when the storm subsides.

_____ 14. To our eyes, the stars move so slowly that we can not tell it.

_____ 15. My sister was glad that she could help you with your trigonometry homework.

_____ 16. The family stood at the end of the lane and peered down the road until the coach could no longer be seen.

_____ 17. Where MacGregor sits, there is the head of the table.

_____ 18. While fighting in France, John was seriously wounded.

_____ 19. As a result of his new medication, my father now breathes more easily than he did before.

_____ 20. The rooms of our old home seemed smaller than I had remembered them.

_____ 21. Mrs. Hawkins has recently moved near her parents so that she can care for them in their old age.

_____ 22. This jacket is so tattered that it should be thrown away.

_____ 23. I did not do well on my persuasive speech because I did not do enough research on the topic.

_____ 24. The preacher spoke longer today than he usually does.

_____ 25. Although the work was hard, the continuous breeze kept us cool throughout the day.

Exercise 51: Dependent Clauses

Underline the verbs twice and the subjects once.
Label all complements (PN, PA, DO, IO, OC, RO).
Put brackets around the dependent clause.
In the left blank, tell whether the dependent clause is used as an adjective clause (ADJ), a noun clause (N), or an adverb clause (ADV).
If the dependent clause is used as an adjective, in the right blank give the noun or pronoun it is modifying.
If the dependent clause is used as an adverb, in the right blank give the verb, adjective, or adverb it is modifying.
If the dependent clause is used as a noun, in the right blank tell how it is used by writing S (subject), PN (predicate nominative), DO (direct object), OP (object of a preposition), etc.

1. As much as lieth in you, live peaceably with all men. —Romans 12:18

2. The powers that be are ordained of God. —Romans 13:1

3. I hope that good seats are still available.

4. When the light changed, naturally I headed forward, through the intersection.

5. The travelers found a place where they could stop for the night.

6. An employee that you can trust is worth his weight in gold.

7. Do you know whether anyone was injured or not?

8. The book to which he referred is *Darwin's Black Box* by Michael Behe.

9. The other team were taller and stronger than we.

10. If I were you, I would leave earlier.

11. The man from whom I received the check did not have sufficient cash in the bank to cover it.

12. He is so tall that he cannot fit comfortably in a compact car.

13. The detectives returned to the spot where the crime had occurred.

14. You may have whichever dessert you want.

15. As the Soviet troops marched west, many people abandoned their homes and fled.

16. My mother does not get out as much as she once did.

17. Donald's plan, that we all contribute a little to a gift for Mrs. Swanson, was acceptable to everyone.

18. I will stay with you until you are feeling better.

19. After the terrorist attack, many journalists and politicians talked about what the future might hold for our country.

20. What we are today is due in large part to the early influences of our lives.

21. The artistic works of Albrecht Durer present a world which is full of life and faith.

22. Jefferson's concerns about the concentration of power in the centralized national government were more prescient than he could have imagined.

Exercise 52: Dependent Clauses

Underline the verbs twice and the subjects once.
Label all complements (PN, PA, DO, IO, OC, RO).
Put brackets around the dependent clause.
In the left blank, tell whether the dependent clause is used as an adjective clause (ADJ), a noun clause (N), or an adverb clause (ADV).
If the dependent clause is used as an adjective, in the right blank give the noun or pronoun it is modifying.
If the dependent clause is used as an adverb, in the right blank give the verb, adjective, or adverb it is modifying.
If the dependent clause is used as a noun, in the right blank tell how it is used by writing S (subject), PN (predicate nominative), DO (direct object), OP (object of a preposition), etc.

____	_____	1.	This article has some good advice for whoever is looking for a job.
____	_____	2.	The land they bought is located near the river.
____	_____	3.	Unfortunately, I cannot do what you ask.
____	_____	4.	We went to the top of the Eiffel Tower, from which we viewed the entire city of Paris.
____	_____	5.	When mortgage rates are high, fewer people can purchase homes.
____	_____	6.	The revolutionaries were confident that the regime would soon topple.
____	_____	7.	In light of current judicial activism, what we can do about abortion seems very unclear.
____	_____	8.	His testimony's lack of concrete details is what is really bothering me.
____	_____	9.	We must work as if everything depends upon us.
____	_____	10.	Marcus was sorry that he could not stay longer.
____	_____	11.	While mowing the yard, I saw a large snake.
____	_____	12.	I stopped her as she was heading out the door.
____	_____	13.	Many of the frontiersmen moved wherever there was good pasture for their herds.
____	_____	14.	He offered a reward to whoever might provide information about the burglary.
____	_____	15.	Joe, you look as if you don't feel well.
____	_____	16.	Those marriages generally abound most with love and constancy that are preceded by a long courtship. —Joseph Addison
____	_____	17.	They that live in a trading street are not disturbed at the passage of carts. —Richard Steele
____	_____	18.	I knew little about the candidate except that he was in favor of a tax increase.
____	_____	19.	The trees which my father set out many years ago now surround our home with shade.
____	_____	20.	Though I walk through the valley of the shadow of death, I will fear no evil. —Psalm 23:4
____	_____	21.	At that point, I was not sure how I would get home.
____	_____	22.	The truck which was carrying our furniture broke down along the way.
____	_____	23.	Do you know where Shakespeare was born?

Exercise 53: Types of Sentences

Locate the verbs, subjects, and complements.
Circle all semicolons or commas and coordinating conjunctions joining independent clauses.
Put brackets around all dependent clauses.
In the blanks at the left, give the number of independent and dependent clauses.
Then tell what type of sentence it is by writing S (simple), CD (compound), CX (complex), or CD-CX (compound-complex).

___ I + ___ D = _____   1.   A little philosophy inclineth man's mind to atheism, but depth in philosophy bringeth men's minds about to religion. —Francis Bacon

___ I + ___ D = _____   2.   The St. John's River flows from south to north and empties into the Atlantic near the Florida-Georgia line. —Marjorie Kinnan Rawlings

___ I + ___ D = _____   3.   Many explorers sought the Northwest Passage, which would give them a direct route to the Orient; however, it was never found.

___ I + ___ D = _____   4.   A truth that's told with bad intent beats all the lies you can invent. —George Herbert

___ I + ___ D = _____   5.   The fruit of the persimmon is at first quite bitter, but later in the season it turns soft and mellow.

___ I + ___ D = _____   6.   If a man does not keep pace with his companions, perhaps it is because he hears a different drummer. —Henry David Thoreau

___ I + ___ D = _____   7.   Hearing the gunshot, the entire flock of birds immediately rose shrieking and cawing.

___ I + ___ D = _____   8.   Would you like to speak to the dean about this matter?

___ I + ___ D = _____   9.   The documentary film which we saw depicted the dangers and importance of Lewis and Clark's expedition across the continent from Missouri to the Pacific and back again.

___ I + ___ D = _____   10.   Many of the bricks that were delivered on Tuesday are either chipped or totally broken; they should be replaced at no additional charge.

___ I + ___ D = _____   11.   I lay down on the sofa for a while, but my headache did not go away.

___ I + ___ D = _____   12.   By the end of the play Hamlet has rejected personal revenge and has taken up the sword of justice.

___ I + ___ D = _____   13.   Michael completed all the problems which his mathematics instructer had assigned.

___ I + ___ D = _____   14.   He opened the door and shouted a greeting to everyone in the room.

___ I + ___ D = _____   15.   I am not really sure that I am qualified for that job.

___ I + ___ D = _____   16.   Mercy and truth are met together; righteousness and peace have kissed each other. —Psalm 85:10

___ I + ___ D = _____   17.   Night's candles are burnt out, and jocund day stands tiptoe on the misty mountaintops. —William Shakespeare

___ I + ___ D = _____   18.   There's a special providence in the fall of a sparrow. —William Shakespeare

Exercise 54: Types of Sentences

Locate the verbs, subjects, and complements.
Circle all semicolons or commas and coordinating conjunctions joining independent clauses.
Put brackets around all dependent clauses.
In the blanks at the left, give the number of independent and dependent clauses.
Then tell what type of sentence it is by writing S (simple), CD (compound), CX (complex), or CD-CX (compound-complex).

___ I + ___ D = _____   1. Throwing his books onto the desk, he flopped down on his bed and sighed deeply.

___ I + ___ D = _____   2. I sometimes feel that a car is merely a necessary evil.

___ I + ___ D = _____   3. A man who will not participate in the electoral process is really not a citizen; he is merely a resident of a country ruled by others.

___ I + ___ D = _____   4. The sergeant gave the command, and the line of soldiers began to move forward.

___ I + ___ D = _____   5. What's mine is yours, and what is yours is mine. —William Shakespeare

___ I + ___ D = _____   6. He that is of a merry heart hath a continual feast. —Proverbs 15:15

___ I + ___ D = _____   7. A day in Thy courts is better than a thousand. —Psalm 84:10

___ I + ___ D = _____   8. If you love everything, you will perceive the divine mystery in things. —Fyodor Dostoevsky

___ I + ___ D = _____   9. The goddess whom the Greeks called Aphrodite went by the name of Venus among the Romans.

___ I + ___ D = _____   10. According to an old legend, the city of Rome was founded by the twin brothers Romulus and Remus.

___ I + ___ D = _____   11. It continued to snow all morning, and by noon the roads were totally impassable.

___ I + ___ D = _____   12. Caesar defeated Pompey; then he gradually took control of the entire Italian peninsula.

___ I + ___ D = _____   13. Dr. Jerkins examined me carefully and then gave me a prescription for an antibiotic.

___ I + ___ D = _____   14. He that covereth his sins shall not prosper, but whoso confesseth and forsaketh them shall have mercy. —Proverbs 28:13

___ I + ___ D = _____   15. Our early settlers frequently left the stumps of trees in their fields; they simply plowed around them.

___ I + ___ D = _____   16. Both printers in the computer laboratory being out of ink, I went to the library.

___ I + ___ D = _____   17. I needed gas, but I was late already.

___ I + ___ D = _____   18. Why are these verbs more irregular than those?

___ I + ___ D = _____   19. Go to the ant, thou sluggard; consider her ways and be wise. —Proverbs 6:6

___ I + ___ D = _____   20. Feeling somewhat ill, I left early.

___ I + ___ D = _____   21. His mother tried to bring down the boy's fever.

___ I + ___ D = _____   22. The cowards never started, and the weak died along the way.

___ I + ___ D = _____   23. In 1937, I began, like Lazarus, the impossible return. —Whittaker Chambers

Exercise 55: Types of Sentences

Locate the verbs, subjects, and complements.
Circle all semicolons or commas and coordinating conjunctions joining independent clauses.
Put brackets around all dependent clauses.
In the blank at the left, tell what type of sentence it is by writing S (simple), CD (compound), CX (complex), or CD-CX (compound-complex).

_____ 1. Oddly, one of the sites in Nashville is a full-scale replica of the ancient Parthenon.

_____ 2. I found several of the books I was looking for, but one of them had already been checked out by someone else.

_____ 3. Men's evil manners live in brass; their virtues we write in water. —William Shakespeare

_____ 4. The terror of atomic weaponry was first made possible by the Manhattan Project, a group of scientists and others working clandestinely during World War II.

_____ 5. How many ages hence shall this our lofty scene be acted o'er, in states unborn and accents yet unknown? —William Shakespeare

_____ 6. The night was absolutely still, with no breeze at all and no moon to be seen.

_____ 7. I had run in several shorter races, but this was my first full marathon.

_____ 8. Whosoever shall exalt himself shall be abased, and he that shall humble himself shall be exalted. —Matthew 23:12

_____ 9. Isn't your brother Howard taller than you?

_____ 10. Cowards die many times before their deaths; the valiant never taste of death but once.
       —William Shakespeare

_____ 11. There is something extremely sad about the lives of those who live forever in cities cut off from pleasures of the woods and the fields.

_____ 12. As I walked through the wilderness of this world, I lighted on a certain place where was a den. —John Bunyan

_____ 13. There was a lady who was besieged by her foes within an earthen castle. —*Ancrene Riwle*

_____ 14. The love of a powerful king was, however, fixed upon her with such boundless affection, that … he sent his ambassadors, one after another. —*Ancrene Riwle*

_____ 15. *The Ancrene Riwle*, an early thirteenth-century manual for nuns, contains the first reference in Western literature to Christ as a knight.

_____ 16. Christ is portrayed allegorically as a knight who comes to the rescue of the human soul and who gives His own life for her deliverance.

_____ 17. Though enemies, the Pharisees and the Sadducees united against Christ.

Exercise 56: Principal Parts of Verbs

In the blanks provided give the present participle, the past, and the past participle of each verb.

present	present participle	past	past participle
1. freeze			
2. love			
3. bring			
4. go			
5. sing			
6. teach			
7. buy			
8. build			
9. occur			
10. ring			
11. think			
12. eat			
13. walk			
14. see			
15. break			
16. grow			
17. pay			
18. honor			
19. choose			
20. write			
21. laugh			
22. plant			
23. swear			
24. lie			
25. raise			

Exercise 57: Irregular Verbs

Underline the correct verb form in the parentheses.

1. The San Francisco Earthquake (occured, occurred) in 1906, I believe.

2. My young brother David fell from a tree and (broke, busted) his left arm.

3. Several burglars (snuck, sneaked) into the museum in Oslo.

4. They (stole, stealed) the painting called *The Scream*, painted by Edvard Munch.

5. I think Earl (did, done) a good job on the landscaping.

6. Sid (lead, led) the horses down to the river for a drink.

7. According to police, several people (seen, saw) the robbery.

8. No, they have already (gone, went) to Lynchburg.

9. The first baseman (threw, throwed) the ball to the catcher for an excellent double play.

10. Overnight several pipes in the Academic Building (bursted, burst), spewing water all over the first floor.

11. As the play (begun, began) several rude latecomers were still finding their seats in the theater.

12. I am convinced that he (knowed, knew) what he did was wrong.

13. My uncle (grew, growed) several extra acres of peanuts this year, but the decline in market prices has defeated his hopes of making some extra money.

14. The dog (dragged, drug) the rug off the porch.

15. We (brought, brung) the groceries into the house and put them on the kitchen counter.

16. The defendant (denyed, denied) that he had had anything to do with the crime.

17. When temperatures suddenly fell below freezing, the oranges in many of the groves were (froze, frozen).

18. The newspaper reported that at least two people had (drownded, drowned) during the hurricane.

19. After the boat capsized, he (swam, swum) to shore.

20. He was sure that the students had (did, done) their best; nevertheless, their low grades were disappointing.

21. When I had (drunk, drank) my usual three cups of coffee, I got up from the breakfast table.

22. We (et, ate) early so that we could go watch the fireworks.

23. Why has he (chose, chosen) to take that course now?

24. The president has (spoken, spoke) on television tonight concerning the terrorist attack.

25. Joel has (wore, worn) his new jacket every day this week.

Exercise 58: Irregular Verbs

Draw a line through any incorrect verb form and write the correct form above it. If a sentence is correct, write C to the left of the number.

1. The hot-water faucet in the bathroom has sprung a leak again.

2. The children have tore several pages out of my history book!

3. Jack came in and, exhausted, sunk, into a chair.

4. When I foolishly washed my sweater, it shrank badly.

5. Mrs. McIntosh shown us how to give CPR.

6. I seen him when he came in last night.

7. She sayed that she had returned the book already.

8. When the bell rung several of the children were not in their seats.

9. Have you written her a thank-you note for the gift?

10. The bloodhounds lead the police to the culprit.

11. Ben done an excellent job on his persuasive speech today.

12. The lifeguard dragged him out of the water and attempted to revive him.

13. Vandals snuck onto the construction site and done several thousand dollars' worth of damage.

14. In Hugo's novel, Jean Valjean stoled the bishop's candlesticks.

15. They brung the car into the shop because the brakes were making a strange noise.

16. We have went to the county fair every year that I can remember.

17. The tour guide showed us where the attack had occurred.

18. My son has grew several inches in the last year.

19. Since it was about to rain, we brought in the clothes from the line.

20. While I was there I boughten myself a new suit.

21. No, sir, I have payed that bill already.

22. The boys swum for a while this afternoon.

23. During the scuffle in the store, several items were broken.

24. After he had finished his chores, he come in for supper.

25. While we were moving, we accidentally busted some of the dishes.

Exercise 59: *Sit* and *Set*

Underline the correct verb form in parentheses.

1. Please (sit, set) down and rest a while, son.

2. He (sat, set) at a table in the library with his books spread in front of him.

3. Mrs. Lawson has (sat, set) out petunias along both sides of the sidewalk.

4. A beautiful bronze statue of Homer (sits, sets) in front of the Classics Building at the University of Virginia.

5. We were (sitting, setting) on the front porch all evening.

6. My mother (sat, set) the two porcelain vases on the mantelpiece.

7. Where should we (sit, set) these pallets while we are unloading them?

8. Does the current governor's mansion (sit, set) on the same site as the earlier one?

9. We are going to (sit, set) the piano in the east end of the living room.

10. Diana (sat, set) a large bouquet of zinnias, marigolds, and daisies on the sideboard in the hall.

11. Mrs. Reid was not sure where in the library to (sit, set) the new periodical shelves.

12. The student body officers will (sit, set) on the stage during the program.

13. I suddenly realized that I was (sitting, setting) in the wrong seat.

14. Don't (sit, set) that hot griddle on the table!

15. Washington ordered several Windsor chairs which he (sat, set) on the piazza at Mount Vernon.

16. The new sofa will (sit, set) over there, opposite the fireplace.

17. Mr. Bilbrey has (sat, set) out several traps for the moles which have been destroying the lawn.

18. Elmington Park (sits, sets) at the corner of West End Avenue and Bowling Street.

19. They have (sat, set) the large display case containing the historical items in the archives room on the second floor.

20. Frank, please (sit, set) Mr. Parrish's things in the guest room.

21. The large unabridged dictionary (sits, sets) on a special desk in the reference room of the library.

22. He (sat, set) at the piano for several seconds and then began to play.

23. A model of the proposed building has been (sit, set) in the lobby of the administration building.

24. He wanted to know where they had (sat, set) all his scientific equipment.

25. They (sat, set) the air conditioner in an upstairs window.

Exercise 60: *Rise* and *Raise*

Underline the correct verb form in parentheses.

1. Christ (rose, raised) from the dead on the third day.

2. Stephen (rose, raised) his hand to ask Miss Phillips a question.

3. As we watched, the large balloon gradually (rose, raised) into the air.

4. At the conclusion of the performance by the drum and fife corps, the soldiers will (rise, raise) the flag.

5. Once again, the flag of Scotland will (raise, rise) over a Scottish parliament.

6. When the upward air thrust under the wings increases, the airplane, of course, (rises, raises).

7. The air trapped in the vessel should cause it to (rise, raise) eventually.

8. The explorers have (risen, raised) the *C.S.S. Hunley* from the floor of Charleston Bay, where it has lain for over a hundred years.

9. Working together, the men were able to (raise, rise) the frame for the new barn.

10. At that point in the ceremony, the choir will (rise, raise) and sing.

11. The space capsule had (risen, raised) high into the atmosphere and had entered orbit around the earth.

12. When the sun had (risen, raised), the travelers began their journey yet again.

13. The weather balloon will (rise, raise) many miles into the atmosphere where it will gather such data as temperature and wind speed.

14. Yet another skyscraper has (risen, raised) over the crowded city.

15. We (rose, raised) from our seats and made our way toward the exit.

16. I am sorry, but I must (rise, raise) my voice in dissent.

17. Each day several of the students in ROTC (rise, raise) the flag on the flagpole in front of the auditorium.

18. Oil from the sunken vessel has continue to (rise, raise) to the surface of the water all these years.

19. King Lear, now quite mad, (rose, raised) his arms and called upon the storm to "strike flat the thick rotundity of the world."

20. Were any objections to the proposal (risen, raised) by any of the county commissioners?

21. In that great getting-up morning, we shall (rise, raise) again.

22. One concern about the location of the highway was (risen, raised) by a local historian.

23. Christians believe that the bodies of the dead will (rise, raise) and be reunited with their souls.

24. The circus "roustabouts," as they were called, (rose, raised) the large pole for the main tent.

25. Livingstone said that he could see the smoke of a thousand villages (rising, raising) into the African sky.

Exercise 61: *Lie* and *Lay*

Underline the correct verb form in parentheses.

1. (Lie, Lay) still and try to sleep, if you can.

2. She (lay, laid) the packages on the kitchen table.

3. On Tuesday morning the workmen will be coming to (lie, lay) the foundation for the addition to our house.

4. Unknown to the world, its Redeemer was, at that moment, (lying, laying) in a cattle trough in a crude barn.

5. The room was a mess; papers were (lying, laying) everywhere.

6. The little fellow (lay, laid) his head on his desk and went to sleep.

7. Tell them to (lie, lay) the roof trusses on the left side of the building.

8. Low in the grave he (lay, laid), Jesus my Saviour. —Robert Lowry

9. (Lie, Lay) your test papers on my desk as you leave.

10. All the hospital rooms being full, the injured had been (laid, lain) on cots in the corridors.

11. Miles below, underneath the earth's crust, (lies, lays) a core of molten rock.

12. Copies of the syllabus were (laying, lying) on the desk at the front of the room.

13. My lazy brother has (lain, laid) in bed all morning.

14. A large yellow cat was (lying, laying) on the hearth.

15. Bags of flour had been (lain, laid) in the storeroom.

16. What is the primary concern that (lies, lays) at the bottom of all these objections?

17. She has (lain, laid) in a hospital bed, in a coma, for three months.

18. The old man (lay, laid) his hand lovingly on the young child's head.

19. A wreath had been (lain, laid) at the Tomb of the Unknown Soldier.

20. The *H.M.S. Titanic* has (lain, laid) at the bottom of the Atlantic since that fateful day in 1912.

21. Bob (lay, laid) his books down on the desk and plopped down on the bed.

22. When Nehemiah returned to Jerusalem, the city (lay, laid) in ruin.

23. After the storm, three large trees were (lying, laying) in our yard, one having crushed my car.

24. The Romans (lay, laid) seige to the city of Jerusalem and finally, in AD 70, destroyed the city, scattering many of its Jewish inhabitants.

25. My father was (lying, laying) in a hammock in the shade.

Exercise 62: Troublesome Verbs

Draw a line through any incorrect verb form and write the correct form above it. If a sentence is correct, write C to the left of the number.

1. The manager sat the cashbox under the counter.

2. All the reporters raised when the president entered the room.

3. In the heat of the afternoon, the cows were laying in the shade, chewing their cud.

4. A group of old men were setting on the bench outside the courthouse.

5. Boy Scouts learn how to raise and lower the flag appropriately.

6. The witness lay his left hand on the Bible and raised his right hand.

7. My mother has been setting out tomatoes in the garden this morning.

8. A wrong belief about the nature of man lies at the heart of many errors of modernity.

9. Christ has risen from the dead and has become "the firstfruits of them that slept."

10. As the judge set down, he immediately called the court into session.

11. The gardener has laid bricks along the edges of all the flower beds.

12. The lioness has laid in her lair with her cubs all day.

13. It is time—and past time—for us to raise up and resist the encroachment of the federal government on the liberties of the states.

14. They picked up the chest and sat it on the wagon.

15. During the afternoon, by working together we were able to raise the walls of the house.

16. I have sat here for over an hour, waiting on you.

17. Ever since its destruction by the Romans, the Temple in Jerusalem has laid in utter ruins, with not one stone upon another.

18. Flames were raising from the roof of the house.

19. Thousands of finches were setting in the branches of the apple trees.

20. A package with your name on it is laying on the dining table.

21. Various objects recovered by the archaeologists have been set here for safekeeping.

22. The old clock, handed down in my father's family, sits on the mantel.

23. The young Roman soldier ran and grabbed the fallen banner and raised it aloft, to the cheers of the troops.

24. A large heap of letters were lying on the table in the mailroom.

25. Where have you lain my screwdriver?

Exercise 63: Verb Tenses

In the blank at the left identify the tense of the italicized verb form by writing present, past, future, present perfect, past perfect, or future perfect.

_____	1. froze	_____	21. is going to attack
_____	2. sings	_____	22. shall hope
_____	3. has told	_____	23. hoped
_____	4. am loving	_____	24. has hoped
_____	5. had washed	_____	25. hopes
_____	6. buy	_____	26. had hoped
_____	7. do know	_____	27. shall have hoped
_____	8. threw	_____	28. is praying
_____	9. is washing	_____	29. was whistling
_____	10. had give	_____	30. will be reading
_____	11. will go	_____	31. has been preaching
_____	12. does believe	_____	32. had been mourning
_____	13. left	_____	33. will have been dwelling
_____	14. will announce	_____	34. does think
_____	15. had remained	_____	35. had had
_____	16. shall have said	_____	36. do have
_____	17. were concocting	_____	37. did receive
_____	18. did build	_____	38. had finished
_____	19. will have shouted	_____	39. has repaired
_____	20. saw	_____	40. have proven

Exercise 64: Verb Tenses

Choose a verb and conjugate it in the spaces provided.

Present Tense (regular)

first person sing.	_____	first person pl.	_____
second person sing.	_____	second person pl.	_____
third person sing.	_____	third person pl.	_____

Present Tense (progressive)

first person sing.	_____	first person pl.	_____
second person sing.	_____	second person pl.	_____
third person sing.	_____	third person pl.	_____

Present Tense (emphatic)

first person sing.	_____	first person pl.	_____
second person sing.	_____	second person pl.	_____
third person sing.	_____	third person pl.	_____

Past Tense (regular)

first person sing.	_____	first person pl.	_____
second person sing.	_____	second person pl.	_____
third person sing.	_____	third person pl.	_____

Past Tense (progressive)

first person sing.	_____	first person pl.	_____
second person sing.	_____	second person pl.	_____
third person sing.	_____	third person pl.	_____

Past Tense (emphatic)

first person sing.	_____	first person pl.	_____
second person sing.	_____	second person pl.	_____
third person sing.	_____	third person pl.	_____

Future Tense (regular)

first person sing.	_____	first person pl.	_____
second person sing.	_____	second person pl.	_____
third person sing.	_____	third person pl.	_____

Future Tense (progressive)

first person sing. _____   first person pl. _____

second person sing. _____   second person pl. _____

third person sing. _____   third person pl. _____

Present Perfect Tense (regular)

first person sing. _____   first person pl. _____

second person sing. _____   second person pl. _____

third person sing. _____   third person pl. _____

Present Perfect Tense (progressive)

first person sing. _____   first person pl. _____

second person sing. _____   second person pl. _____

third person sing. _____   third person pl. _____

Past Perfect Tense (regular)

first person sing. _____   first person pl. _____

second person sing. _____   second person pl. _____

third person sing. _____   third person pl. _____

Past Perfect Tense (progressive)

first person sing. _____   first person pl. _____

second person sing. _____   second person pl. _____

third person sing. _____   third person pl. _____

Future Perfect Tense (regular)

first person sing. _____   first person pl. _____

second person sing. _____   second person pl. _____

third person sing. _____   third person pl. _____

Future Perfect Tense (progressive)

first person sing. _____   first person pl. _____

second person sing. _____   second person pl. _____

third person sing. _____   third person pl. _____

Exercise 65: Tense Sequence

Underline the verb form in parentheses which best expresses the logical time sequence in the sentence.

1. When April (finished, had finished) her research, she began writing her paper.

2. When the president and first lady (entered, had entered) the room, the Marine band began to play "Hail to the Chief."

3. If Donna (would have practiced, had practiced) more, she would have performed better in the recital.

4. (Looking, Having looked) out the window, they could see the crowd gathering on the street.

5. The biologists were eager (to find out, to have found out) the results of the experiment.

6. All the passengers were glad (to reach, to have reached) their destination safe and sound.

7. (Doing, Having done) the best I could on the entrance examination, I returned home to await my scores.

8. If the car (would have started, had started), I would have been here on time.

9. (Seeing, Having seen) herself in the mirror, Christine admired her new dress.

10. Our family has been wanting (to invite, to have invited) you to our house for a long time.

11. (Hearing, Having heard) the bell, I knew I was late for my third-period class.

12. Donald said that he (left, had left) his term paper in his room.

13. When he (consulted, had consulted) many census figures and tax records, Frank Owsley was able to give an accurate depiction of the "plain folk of the Old South" as he called them.

14. After the firefighters (put, had put) out the blaze, inspectors from the fire marshall's office began to inspect the premises.

15. (Suspecting, Having suspected) arson, they searched the building carefully for evidence.

16. When I (saw, had seen) the monoliths at Stonehenge, I was amazed at their size and at the ingenuity of their construction.

17. I hope (to get, to have gotten) an early start tomorrow morning.

18. When I (vacuumed, had vacuumed) the carpet, I put the furniture back where it belonged.

19. At their family's roadside stand, Jeff and Susan sold the peaches which they (picked, had picked) early that morning.

20. (Finishing, Having finished) his tour of duty overseas, my brother was transferred to a base in the United States.

21. The library assistant intended (to reshelve, to have reshelved) the books after she logged them back in on the computer.

22. Douglas said that he was sorry (to miss, to have missed) your performance on Saturday.

23. When the storm (ended, had ended), we went outside to survey the damage.

24. (Looking, Having looked) at the clock, Bridget knew that she was late.

25. (Leaning, Having leaned) over the balcony, I could see the pedestrians, like ants, on the sidewalk below.

Exercise 66: Tense Sequence

Draw a line through any incorrect verb form and write the correct form above it. If a sentence is correct, write C to the left of the number.

1. Dr. Fisher, our chemistry teacher, thought that he adequately explained what we were to do.

2. Not hearing any convincing evidence, the judge ordered the man to be released.

3. If you would have measured each of the ingredients carefully, the result might have been different.

4. When the official gave the signal, the runners immediately raced forward.

5. Eating something that did not agree with him, he got a bad stomach ache.

6. Several students were planning to see the production of *A Comedy of Errors* at Centennial Park.

7. When he read his text, the young minister paused and then started his brief sermon.

8. If the other members of my group would have done their work, we would have gotten a better grade on our panel discussion.

9. Seeing the clouds in the sky, my father recommended that we postpone the picnic.

10. My car breaking down, I had no way to get home.

11. The police having discovered several things that connected him with the crime, he was formally charged.

12. The reapers, working steadily for several hours, sat down for a rest and something to eat and drink.

13. If the French would not have helped us in the Revolutionary War, would we have won?

14. We were eager to see their production of *Fiddler on the Roof.*

15. As soon as he graded several of the papers, Professor Tilton knew that something was wrong.

16. The young girl, who was so near death earlier, now was sitting up in bed and speaking.

17. The academic dean told me that he mailed me several letters asking for the information.

18. Seeing the chocolate cake that my wife had made, I just could not resist having a piece—or two.

19. If the building had been constructed properly, these cracks in the foundation would not have formed.

20. The sailors were thankful to have come through the storm alive.

21. After we finished our tour of the Smithsonian Institute, we went to the National Gallery of Art.

22. The policeman pointed out to me that my parking meter had expired.

23. Copying the passage of the *Aeneid* in my notebook, I then looked up each of the words in my Latin dictionary.

24. Watching the snow falling, I lost all track of time.

25. We were glad that we finished the roof before the rain.

Exercise 67: Active and Passive Voice

Underline the verbs twice and the subjects once.
Label all complements (PN, PA, DO, IO, OC, RO).
In the blank at the left identify the voice of the verb by writing TA-AV (transitive active action verb),
TP-AV (transitive passive action verb), I-AV (intransitive action verb), or LV (linking verb).

_____ 1. Not long after lunch I became quite ill.

_____ 2. An aunt of mine gave me several photographs of my father as a child.

_____ 3. After my initial letter of inquiry, I was sent some brochures about job opportunities in Peru.

_____ 4. Three children were running around the classroom.

_____ 5. Kate Chopin called her shocking feminist novel *The Awakening*.

_____ 6. Screaches of hawks and owls could be heard down on the valley floor.

_____ 7. On a cold winter day, a bowl of hot vegetable soup tastes delicious.

_____ 8. Esau, a profane man, sold his birthright to his brother Jacob.

_____ 9. In Chaucer's *Canterbury Tales* we have been left a very descriptive picture of the medieval world.

_____ 10. Abraham traveled from his home in Ur, in the land of Sumer, to Canaan, near the Mediterranean Sea.

_____ 11. The young firefighter was awarded a medal for his bravery on the fateful day of the terrorist attack.

_____ 12. The nurse handed the surgeon a pair of forceps.

_____ 13. A long rattlesnake was lying on the bottom step in the sun.

_____ 14. The secretary laid the folders on Mr. Caruthers's desk.

_____ 15. In the Epistle to the Hebrews the Jewish Christians are warned about the danger of spiritual apostasy.

_____ 16. Martin Luther nailed his Ninety-five Theses to the church door in the German town of Wittenburg.

_____ 17. In these animal paintings by Albrecht Durer the value of the physical world of creation can be clearly seen.

_____ 18. During the inteview the reporter was told several things about the president's trip to Poland.

_____ 19. The church's teaching on human sexuality has remained remarkably consistent throughout the entire two-thousand-year history of the church.

_____ 20. In most countries throughout the former British Empire, the game of cricket is very popular.

_____ 21. All the students have been given a copy of the college's policy on drugs and alcohol.

_____ 22. George Eliot's novels often reveal a real nostalgia for the pre-industrial world.

_____ 23. Juliet was given a sleeping potion by Friar Lawrence.

_____ 24. During the earthquake, many buildings in Tokyo were damaged.

_____ 25. This decision certainly seems sudden!

Exercise 68: Passive Voice

Choose a transitive action verb and conjugate it in passive voice in the spaces provided.

Present Tense (regular)

first person sing. _____   first person pl. _____

second person sing. _____   second person pl. _____

third person sing. _____   third person pl. _____

Present Tense (progressive)

first person sing. _____   first person pl. _____

second person sing. _____   second person pl. _____

third person sing. _____   third person pl. _____

Past Tense (regular)

first person sing. _____   first person pl. _____

second person sing. _____   second person pl. _____

third person sing. _____   third person pl. _____

Past Tense (progressive)

first person sing. _____   first person pl. _____

second person sing. _____   second person pl. _____

third person sing. _____   third person pl. _____

Future Tense (regular)

first person sing. _____   first person pl. _____

second person sing. _____   second person pl. _____

third person sing. _____   third person pl. _____

Present Perfect Tense (regular)

first person sing. _____   first person pl. _____

second person sing. _____   second person pl. _____

third person sing. _____   third person pl. _____

Past Perfect Tense (regular)

first person sing. _____   first person pl. _____

second person sing. _____   second person pl. _____

third person sing. _____   third person pl. _____

Future Perfect Tense (regular)

first person sing.	_____	first person pl.	_____
second person sing.	_____	second person pl.	_____
third person sing.	_____	third person pl.	_____

Exercise 69: Active and Passive Voice

Underline the verbs twice and the subjects once.
Label all complements (PN, PA, DO, IO, OC, RO).
In the blank at the left identify the voice of the verb by writing TA-AV (transitive active action verb),
TP-AV (transitive passive-action verb), I-AV (intransitive action verb), or LV (linking verb).

_____	1.	According to the Greeks, before the creation of man the earth was inhabited by the Titans.
_____	2.	Mankind was given the gift of fire by Prometheus, one of those Titans.
_____	3.	By the disobedience of Pandora, evils of all sorts were loosed upon the world.
_____	4.	The classical story of the lovers Pyramus and Thisbe offered Shakespeare the model for his Romeo and Juliet.
_____	5.	The holiday of Saturnalia in the ancient world commemmorated the reign of Saturn in the "golden age."
_____	6.	The god Apollo drove his golden chariot across the heavens each day.
_____	7.	Despite his noblest efforts, young Phaeton, Apollo's son, "could not rule his father's car of fire."
_____	8.	Men could be turned to stone by one glance of the awful Medusa.
_____	9.	Jason and his men sailed their ship the *Argo* in search of the Golden Fleece.
_____	10.	Legend calls these heroes and companions of Jason the Argonauts.
_____	11.	As a youth, I was read these stories from the famous book on mythology by Thomas Bulfinch.
_____	12.	The gods gave Hercules twelve difficult tasks.
_____	13.	Hercules was allotted these labors because of the hatred of Juno.
_____	14.	Atlas, one of the Titans, bore the weight of the world on his shoulders.
_____	15.	The golden apples in the garden of the Hesperides have become famous.
_____	16.	Atalanta was finally defeated in a footrace by Hippomenes.
_____	17.	Queen Hippolyta ruled the Amazons, a tribe of warlike women.
_____	18.	The Minotaur was fed human victims from Athens.
_____	19.	The hero Theseus had made his way through the mysterious labyrinth to the monster.
_____	20.	For his brave exploit, Theseus was awarded the throne of Athens.
_____	21.	Youths from all over Greece participated in the Olympic games.
_____	22.	The winner of an athletic or artistic contest was presented a wreath of laurel leaves, in honor of Apollo.
_____	23.	Aeneas and his kin were escaping from the city of Troy.
_____	24.	He married the Italian beauty Lavinia.
_____	25.	The city of Rome was founded by their descendants.

Exercise 70: Moods

In the blank at the left identify the mood of the italicized verb form by writing IND (indicative), IMP (imperative), or SUBJ (subjunctive).

_____ 1. We *understand* a literary text from the meaning of its words and from the historical context of those words.

_____ 2. *Did* you *study* a foreign language in high school?

_____ 3. *Look* through the telescope and describe the surface of the moon.

_____ 4. If you *cannot see* clearly, adjust the mechanism here.

_____ 5. If he *were* governor, he would tighten the budget and reduce government expenses.

_____ 6. Marco Polo *visited* the court of Kubla Khan in China in the thirteenth century.

_____ 7. He looked as if he *were* ill.

_____ 8. *Have* you *given* any thought to what you will do after graduation?

_____ 9. The optometrist asked me if I *was* able to read the top line on the chart.

_____ 10. The books looked as though they *were* very old.

_____ 11. In chapel on Tuesday, the College Choir *sang* an anthem by John Rutter.

_____ 12. I wish I *were* better *prepared* for this test.

_____ 13. As I *turned* the key in the ignition, nothing happened.

_____ 14. If she *should get* the role of Cordelia, she would do an excellent job.

_____ 15. The physician asked that the nurse *give* the patient an injection of morphine.

_____ 16. The witness acted as though he *were* unsure what to say.

_____ 17. Mr. Chairman, I make a motion that we *cease* nominations and go immediately to the vote.

_____ 18. The attorney requested that the court reporter *read* the witness's previous response.

_____ 19. The judge ruled that the defendant *be held* without bond.

_____ 20. It was ordered that Haman *be hanged* on the gallows that he had built for Mordecai.

_____ 21. Despite our best efforts, we *lost* the last game of the tournament.

_____ 22. What will they do if it *should rain*?

_____ 23. Chivalry dictates that a gentleman *open* a door for a lady.

_____ 24. When you have completed the application form, *give* it to the secretary.

_____ 25. What *were* the dimensions of the building originally?

Exercise 71: Subjunctive Mood

Underline the verb form in parentheses which expresses the necessary subjunctive mood.

1. What would he do differently if he (was, were) in charge?

2. If I (was, were) able, I would loan you the money, Will.

3. One of the students kept piping up to give his opinion, as if he (was, were) the instructor.

4. For his own protection, Hamlet acted as though he (was, were) insane.

5. I wish that the situation (was, were) different and that I might help you.

6. The academic dean requested that each faculty member (give, gives) him a copy of his syllabus.

7. King Charles I demanded that Parliament (submits, submit) to his authority.

8. Samantha made a motion that the meeting (be, is) adjourned until next week.

9. The judge issued a writ of habeas corpus and ordered that the prosecutor either (charge, charges) the defendants or release them.

10. The poor old horse looked as if it (was, were) about to fall down under the weight of its load.

11. Since she has no insurance, I don't know what she would do if she (was, were) seriously ill.

12. If your mother (was, were) aware of your actions, she would certainly not approve.

13. Dr. Harbison suggested that I (be, am) permitted to look into the matter.

14. The speaker of the House demanded that the House of Commons (comes, come) to order.

15. The college requires that each student (takes, take) the Scholastic Aptitude Test before admission.

16. His parents insisted that he (tells, tell) them exactly how the accident happened.

17. The potential buyer requested that a response to his offer (be, is) made by next Friday.

18. The band director insists that Allan (practices, practice) his tuba everyday.

19. If Jenni (was, were) willing to be treasurer, I would be glad to nominate her.

20. I wish that it (was, were) summer already.

21. The attorney requested that the judge (grant, grants) a continuance so that he could have more time to prepare his case.

22. After listening to the arguments, Judge Denson ruled that the case (be, is) dismissed.

23. Deborah was quite pale; she looked as if she (was, were) getting sick.

24. I wish this assignment (was, were) not so long.

25. His roommate requested that he (keeps, keep) his things put away.

Exercise 72: Subject-Verb Agreement

Underline the subject of the verb.
Underline the verb form in parentheses which agrees with the subject.

1. A row of trees (stands, stand) in the median on Richland Avenue.

2. The greatest benefit of the garden, I suppose, (is, are) fresh, homegrown tomatoes.

3. There (has, have) been several robberies in this area within the last week.

4. Here (is, are) the information you requested.

5. The Bahamas (is, are) a nation comprising over seven hundred different islands in the South Atlantic.

6. *The Canterbury Tales* (includes, include) such diverse works as the philosophical "Knight's Tale," the melodramatic "Prioress's Tale," and a sermon on penance by the parson.

7. (Does, Do) Bartlett's *Familiar Quotations* contain any quotations from films?

8. There (seems, seem) to be several discrepancies between these two financial audits.

9. C. S. Lewis's *Chronicles of Narnia* (attempts, attempt) to give a picture—in fantasy—of the Christian view of atonement and redemption.

10. Here (stands, stand) the Cenotaph, a monument to the thousands of British dead in World War I.

11. (Isn't, Aren't) Niagara Falls located on the American-Canadian border?

12. The president, along with several of his primary advisors, (is, are) meeting with other NATO leaders in Brussels.

13. Grovers Corners (is, are) the fictional setting for the play *Our Town*.

14. A hedge of cedar trees (marks, mark) the western boundary.

15. There (was, were) three ships in Columbus's fleet during his first voyage in 1492.

16. Even though set in outlandish places inhabited by Lilliputians and talking horses, *Gulliver's Travels* actually (depicts, depict) many of the problems of eighteenth-century Britain.

17. The main agricultural crop of the state of Washington (is, are) apples.

18. Strauss's *Tales from the Vienna Woods* (was, were) performed by the Philadelphia Orchestra last night.

19. (Isn't, Aren't) *The Boys from Syracuse* based on Shakespeare's *Comedy of Errors*?

20. A row of stately oak trees (was, were) leading up to the front door of the old plantation house.

21. The governor, along with several local officials, (has, have) visited the areas hardest hit by the hurricane.

22. To most observers, Victoria Falls (presents, present) an amazing spectacle.

23. The water dropping hundreds of feet down into the valley below, together with the glories of the African wilderness, (is, are) truly awe-inspiring.

24. (Isn't, Aren't) Shaker Heights now a suburb of Cleveland?

25. Where (is, are) the boxes you brought in?

Exercise 73: Subject-Verb Agreement

Underline the subject of the verb.
Underline the verb form in parentheses which agrees with the subject.

1. In children, rickets (is, are) usually accompanied by defective bone growth.

2. The Admissions Committee (has, have), unfortunately, rejected your application.

3. To begin their deliberations, the jury (was, were) expressing their opinions about the case.

4. Two thirds of the houses in our community (was, were) severely damaged by the tornado.

5. To me, seventy five dollars (seems, seem) too much to pay for even a good pair of shoes.

6. As a result of the late rain, three fourths of the cotton crop (has, have) been lost.

7. In high school, physics (was, were) probably my most difficult course.

8. Despite the building's beauty, the acoustics of the new auditorium (is, are) quite bad.

9. Upon inspection, we discovered that twenty-five percent of the imported tiles (was, were) cracked or broken.

10. In my youth, measles (was, were) still quite common.

11. The panel of experts (has, have) expressed their doubts concerning the document's authenticity.

12. At commencement, the faculty (sit, sits) on the stage.

13. The lawyer's verbal pyrotechnics (was, were) not able to change the facts of the case.

14. Fourteen instances of leukemia (seems, seem) to be a large number for such a small community; perhaps we can determine a common cause.

15. In recent years, genetics (has, have) received more attention as a result of discoveries related to DNA.

16. During the Battle of New Orleans, the American army (was, were) able to rout the British.

17. The athletes' gymnastics (was, were) certainly enjoyed by the audience in the Olympic stadium; over and over, the crowd erupted in prolonged cheers.

18. Three fifths of the sugar produced in this country (is, are) made from sugar cane.

19. Seventeen gold doubloons (has, have) been recovered from the hull of the wrecked vessel.

20. AIDS (results, result) in the inability of the immune system to resist disease.

21. Eighty-five percent of the courses in the English Department (is, are) three-hour courses.

22. The techtonics of the earth's crust (is, are) what leads to earthquakes.

23. The City Council (holds, hold) its monthly meeting on the first Tuesday of each month.

24. The City Council (was, were) unable to agree on what they wanted to do about the recent rise in burglaries.

25. Civics (gives, give) students an appreciation for how our government works.

Exercise 74: Subject-Verb Agreement

Underline the subject of the verb.
Underline the verb form in parentheses which agrees with the subject.

1. San Francisco and Oakland (is, are) located across the bay from one another.

2. The lieutenant governor and the president of the Senate (is, are) Sam Reilly.

3. Either the dean of students or one of the resident directors (is, are) always on duty in case of an emergency.

4. Neither the chairmen of the academic departments nor the academic dean (was, were) supportive of the proposed changes in the grading scale.

5. The secretary of defense or his assistants (is, are) going to speak to reporters after the meeting.

6. Both the chief justice and the other members of the Supreme Court (serves, serve) indefinite terms.

7. The secretary and treasurer of Alpha Chi Omega (is, are) Patrick Dawson.

8. Mr. Godwin or another of the bank managers (has, have) scheduled to meet with us.

9. Allen Tate and the other Agrarian authors (was, were) concerned about the materialist views then prominent in American society.

10. Neither Washington nor the other "Founding Fathers" (was, were) in favor of an irreligious or morally neutral government.

11. Either my parents or my Uncle John (is, are) going to accompany me on my visit to the campus.

12. The president and CEO of the corporation (is, are) Arthur Forbes.

13. Stock brokers and bankers (needs, need) a thorough education in economics and investment practices.

14. Dr. Jones, along with several students from the Biblical Studies Department, (is, are) going to attend the conference in Louisville.

15. Where (is, are) those books I ordered?

16. There (is, are) several possible explanations for the cause of the fire .

17. *Six Crises* (offers, offer) a glimpse into the early political career of Richard Nixon.

18. Since the nineteenth century Eureka Springs (has, have) remained a popular tourist site in Arkansas.

19. Small-pox (is, are) accompanied by high fever, body ache, and blisters.

20. The State Game Commission (sets, set) the dates for the various hunting seasons in the state.

21. During the meeting, the school board (has, have) expressed their opinions about the proposed textbooks.

22. After the unexpected attack, two thirds of the ships (was, were) severely damaged or destroyed.

23. Cryogenics (is, are) the study of the effects produced by extremely low temperatures.

24. In my opinion, thirty thousand dollars (is, are) an exorbitant price for a car.

25. Here (is, are) the receipts you wanted.

Exercise 75: Subject-Verb Agreement

Underline the subject of the verb.
Underline the verb form in parentheses which agrees with the subject.

1. Somebody (has, have) left an umbrella in the hall.

2. Each of the members of the panel (is, are) going to discuss a different cause of the war.

3. Both of the speakers (has, have) supported the resolution.

4. During the battle, many of the soldiers (was, were) badly wounded.

5. As a result of the leak in the roof, some of the books (was, were) damaged.

6. It was later discovered that some of the information (was, were) incorrect.

7. In my opinion, Ryan (doesn't, don't) really understand the situation.

8. Everyone (was, were) glad to see our old friends again.

9. No, none of these shirts (is, are) the right size.

10. Several of the computers (is, are) off-line for some reason.

11. It certainly (wasn't, weren't) the result which I had predicted.

12. Most of these paintings (was, were) given to the museum in the late nineteenth century.

13. When I arrived, nobody (was, were) there.

14. Several of the students (was, were) absent because of the basketball tournament.

15. (Does, Do) most of the oil used in the United States come from outside the country?

16. All of Dostoevsky's novels (raises, raise) provocative theological questions.

17. (Wasn't, Weren't) they in Australia last summer?

18. In my opinion, neither of the candidates (is, are) offering a real solution to the problem of illegal immigration.

19. During the meeting, everyone (was, were) free to contribute his views.

20. No, I (wasn't, weren't) there on Tuesday.

21. Several copies of Grantham's book (is, are) available in Welch Library.

22. As a result of the increase in the price of gasoline, some of us (has, have) decided to buy smaller cars.

23. (Has, Have) either of the physicians discovered the cause of her paralysis?

24. My brother (doesn't, don't) live in Vermont anymore.

25. (Is, Are) any of these dictionaries included on the list of required textbooks?

Exercise 76: Subject-Verb Agreement

Draw a line through any verb form which does not agree with its subject and write the correct form above it. If a sentence is correct, write C to the left of the number.

1. The most important consideration, in my opinion, is the many people who will be left unemployed.
2. A list of grades has been posted on Dr. Reid's office door.
3. Tennyson's *Idylls of the King* tell the story of King Arthur and the knights of the Round Table.
4. Where's the paper towels?
5. The governor, together with the heads of several cabinet-level departments, are meeting today with the residents of Manchester.
6. Some of Frost's poems present the moral dilemmas of modernity.
7. Measles is usually accompanied by an outbreak of red spots all over the body.
8. At the conclusion of the hearing, the County Commission was still unwilling to give its assent to the zoning change.
9. To me, $150 seem a high price for one pair of pants.
10. Only two thirds of the students has received their immunizations.
11. The graphics available on this computer program are certainly going to improve our presentation.
12. James Thomson and Thomas Gray present a decided change from the earlier Neoclassical poets.
13. The founder and president of our company are Gerald Hawkins.
14. Neither my professors nor the academic dean were able to answer my question satisfactorily.
15. Here is the files you requested, Mr. Campbell.
16. Both Katherine and her parents are planning to visit the campus in November.
17. Surely somebody was responsible for taking minutes at the meeting.
18. Many homes were severely damaged in the recent hurricane.
19. Two thirds of the sugar cane was destroyed as well.
20. This calculator don't work properly.
21. Several of Rembrandt's paintings depicts Jewish residents of Amsterdam.
22. There is no easy answers to Mrs. Calderon's questions.
23. Either President Pinson or the deans is going to be present at the next meeting of the Student Council.
24. The influence of Darwin, Nietzsche, and Freud were able to change the philosophical basis of Western culture.
25. Don't he attend a university in California?

Exercise 77: Personal Pronoun Cases

In the left blank, tell how the personal pronoun is used by writing S (subject), PN (predicate nominative), DO (direct object), IO (indirect object), OP (object of a preposition), S-INF (subject of an infinitive), POSS (possessive before a gerund), etc. In the right blank, give the personal pronoun case that should be used: NOM (nominative), OBJ (objective), or POSS (possessive).
Underline the correct case form of the personal pronoun in parentheses.

_____ _____ 1. Charlie and (I, me) worked on our project for history class together.

_____ _____ 2. The blame for the mix-up lies squarely with Arty and (I, me).

_____ _____ 3. Mrs. Hawley gave Theresa and (she, her) permission to leave class early in order to set up for the symposium.

_____ _____ 4. She thanked (we, us) boys for cleaning up her yard.

_____ _____ 5. The owner of the property is (he, him).

_____ _____ 6. My father wanted (I, me) to finish my chores before leaving.

_____ _____ 7. (We, Us) citizens must express our opinions to our elected representatives.

_____ _____ 8. The nursing home administrator said that she certainly appreciated (we, us, our) visiting today.

_____ _____ 9. When you have completed the application form, please give it to Miss McElhinney or (I, me).

_____ _____ 10. The old man picked up his fiddle and played a tune for Addie and (they, them).

_____ _____ 11. As you enter the library please give Mrs. Hampton and (she, her) your completed worksheet.

_____ _____ 12. (He, Him, His) raising that question about the costs of the project certainly prolonged the discussion.

_____ _____ 13. Do you wish Tommy and (I, me) to open these boxes, Mr. Schmidt?

_____ _____ 14. The preacher at the morning service will be (he, him).

_____ _____ 15. At that crucial moment in the story, Faithful and (he, him) visit the city of Vanity Fair.

_____ _____ 16. The wicked rulers of Vanity Fair captured Christian and (he, him) and put them on trial.

_____ _____ 17. Yes, Bridget and (I, me) were told this by an eyewitness.

_____ _____ 18. My objections to (you, your) driving the van are not personal.

_____ _____ 19. General Gage and (they, them) were soundly routed at the Battle of Saratoga.

_____ _____ 20. Mrs. Yoder would like (we, us) girls to be at work by 7:30.

_____ _____ 21. Before the test, Miss Callaway asked (we, us) students several questions about dependent clauses.

_____ _____ 22. In my opinion, (he, him, his) working such long hours may, eventually, affect his family.

_____ _____ 23. Do you think that Ian sings better than (he, him)?

_____ _____ 24. Yes, (we, us) voters are very concerned about the current moral climate of the nation.

_____ _____ 25. Do you want (she, her) to set the table now?

Exercise 78: Personal Pronoun Cases

In the left blank, tell how the personal pronoun is used by writing S (subject), PN (predicate nominative), DO (direct object), IO (indirect object), OP (object of a preposition), S-INF (subject of an infinitive), POSS (possessive before a gerund), etc. In the right blank, give the personal pronoun case that should be used: NOM (nominative), OBJ (objective), or POSS (possessive).
Underline the correct case form of the personal pronoun in parentheses.

_____ _____ 1. Ben and (she, her) performed a scene from *The Crucible*.

_____ _____ 2. The delightful roles of Benedict and Beatrice were given to Sam and (she, her).

_____ _____ 3. One problem during the production was (he, him, his) turning on the spotlight too early in the second act.

_____ _____ 4. Did anyone see (he, him, his) standing behind the curtain?

_____ _____ 5. Mr. Bradley urged Howard and (they, them) to speak more loudly.

_____ _____ 6. Clearly, the ones who performed best were Katie and (she, her).

_____ _____ 7. (We, Us) members of the cast have a small gift for you, sir.

_____ _____ 8. The director and (she, her) were obviously happy with tonight's rehearsal.

_____ _____ 9. As you leave, please give Anna and (he, him) your copies of the script.

_____ _____ 10. In the last scene of the play, Laertes and (he, him) apologize to one another.

_____ _____ 11. The roles played by David and (they, them) required a real sensitivity.

_____ _____ 12. After the last performance, Mrs. Pinson gave a party for (we, us) performers and stage hands.

_____ _____ 13. In this scene, Lady Macbeth and (he, him) discuss the murder of King Duncan.

_____ _____ 14. Due to recent fiscal problems, the treasurer wants (we, us) to cut back to only two dramatic productions a year.

_____ _____ 15. We certainly appreciate (you, your) coming to the play tonight; we hope you enjoy it.

_____ _____ 16. I really enjoyed (they, them, their) singing "Matchmaker, Matchmaker."

_____ _____ 17. Did you see Jennifer and (he, him, his) passing out programs at the front door?

_____ _____ 18. Next spring Mr. Payne and (they, them) will be presenting *The Sound of Music*.

_____ _____ 19. The ones with the most lines are Daniel and (she, her), who play Petruchio and Katharina.

_____ _____ 20. Not attending rehearsals regularly and promptly will result, unfortunately, in (you, your) being cut from the cast.

_____ _____ 21. Is Victor taller than (she, her)?

_____ _____ 22. The stage hands were (he, him) and Brian.

_____ _____ 23. The roles of Tevye and his wife Golde were played by Andrew and (she, her).

_____ _____ 24. The high point of *The Miracle Worker* is (she, her) learning to spell *water*.

_____ _____ 25. Please give Doug and (I, me) your tickets.

Exercise 79: *Who* and *Whom*

In the left blank, tell how the pronoun is used by writing S (subject), PN (predicate nominative), DO (direct object), IO (indirect object), OP (object of a preposition), etc.
In the right blank, give the pronoun case that should be used: NOM (nominative), OBJ (objective), or POSS (possessive).
Underline the correct case form of the pronoun in parentheses.

_____ _____ 1. By (who, whom) was the United States Capitol designed?

_____ _____ 2. (Who, Whom) did you give the package to?

_____ _____ 3. (Who, Whom) did he say was elected treasurer?

_____ _____ 4. The gentleman with (who, whom) she spoke gave her a copy of the schedule.

_____ _____ 5. The baskets of food will be given to (whoever, whomever) needs them.

_____ _____ 6. Do you know (who's, whose) coat this is?

_____ _____ 7. I shall hire (whoever, whomever) you recommend.

_____ _____ 8. (Who, Whom) was she walking with?

_____ _____ 9. The property was sold to (who, whom)?

_____ _____ 10. After the year had passed, Sir Gawain began his search for the Green Knight, (who, whom) he had promised to fight with.

_____ _____ 11. That fellow (who's, whose) standing next to Nathaniel is my cousin Jack.

_____ _____ 12. (Who, Whom) the Lord loveth He chasteneth. —Hebrews 12:6

_____ _____ 13. (Whoever, Whomever) we elect must be a person of character.

_____ _____ 14. (Who, Whom) does he sit beside in calculus class?

_____ _____ 15. The man or woman (who, whom) we choose needs a good understanding of the arts.

_____ _____ 16. (Whoever, Whomever) wants to go with us should let us know today.

_____ _____ 17. To (who, whom) did your grandfather leave his farm?

_____ _____ 18. (Who, Whom) did your sister marry?

_____ _____ 19. The secretary to (who, whom) she gave the envelope failed to put it in the mail.

_____ _____ 20. (Who's, Whose) woods these are I think I know. —Robert Frost

_____ _____ 21. (Who's, Whose) the owner of this red Corvette?

_____ _____ 22. (Who, Whom) did Samuel anoint to be king of Israel?

_____ _____ 23. (Who, Whom) did Coach Higgins want to be the captain of the soccer team?

_____ _____ 24. The retiring schoolteacher offered his bulletin board materials to (whoever, whomever) wanted them.

_____ _____ 25. (Who, Whom) did you ask to the concert, Joe?

Exercise 80: Pronoun-Antecedent Agreement

In the blank at the left, give the antecedent of the pronoun.
Underline the pronoun which agrees with that antecedent.

1. Someone has parked (his, their) car in a fire zone.
2. Several of the buildings had lost (its, their) shingles in the storm.
3. Some of society's problems have (its, their) source in a wrong concept of human nature.
4. Some of this poetry uses iambic pentameter for (its, their) metrical pattern.
5. Hugh and Seth often give (his, their) time to the Rescue Mission.
6. Neither Lyle nor his brother has turned in (his, their) application.
7. Both Dr. Armand and Dr. House have (his, their) offices in the new Physicians Building on Maxwell Street.
8. Neither the pastor nor the deacons had given (his, their) opinions about the proposal.
9. Either Jason or his roommates will be present to express (his, their) objections.
10. Percherons are a type of horse which is raised for (its, their) ability to pull wagons or other farm equipment.
11. I would like to thank those ladies who contributed (her, their) efforts to this worthy project.
12. The large maple tree in our yard has already lost most of (its, his) leaves.
13. The ewe became quite upset when we came too close to (its, her) lambs.
14. The ram also became angry, tossing (its, his) horns menacingly.
15. A goose serves as a good guard; (he, it) will begin to squawk when visitors approach.
16. A good physician will spend time with (his or her, their) patients, learning as much about them and their lives as possible.
17. Everybody needs to turn in (his, their) research paper outline.
18. A lawyer must remember (his, their) obligation to seek the public good not merely private gain.
19. Several teachers placed (his or her, their) textbook lists and syllabi on-line.
20. No one has permission to remove college furniture from (his, their) dormitory room.
21. Most of the farmers tilled (his, their) fields with great care.
22. Everybody except Dale turned in (his, their) outline.
23. Either Mrs. Reid or the library assistants will give us (her, their) help in our research.
24. Did the mare seem to mind your touching (his, her, its) foal?
25. A voter may take (his or her, their) young children into the voting booth.

Exercise 81: Pronoun-Antecedent Agreement

In the blank at the left, give the antecedent of the pronoun.
Underline the pronoun which agrees with that antecedent.

_____ 1. Everyone should bring (his, their) book to class everyday.

_____ 2. Donald Cheng and his brother talked to the students about (his, their) experiences in Communist China.

_____ 3. Neither the governor nor the senators have given (his, their) support to the bill.

_____ 4. Recently in our city, a German shepherd was given a citation for bravery for saving the life of (his, its) master.

_____ 5. Neither Jared nor Tom remembered to request a copy of (his, their) transcript.

_____ 6. Do you know the gentlemen who recently donated (his, their) books to the college?

_____ 7. The old book had lost (its, his) cover, and many of the pages were torn.

_____ 8. Several of the soldiers would suffer from (his, their) wounds for many years to come.

_____ 9. Both April and Sarah are prepared to give (her, their) speeches today.

_____ 10. Neither my brothers nor my father wanted to change (his, their) clothes, but my mother insisted.

_____ 11. How long does a hen sit on (its, her) eggs before they hatch?

_____ 12. In Aesop's fable, the rooster, called Chanticleer, is captured by the fox after (he, it) is duped into crowing.

_____ 13. Pericles was one of the Greeks who became famous for (his, their) oratory.

_____ 14. Cast your vote only after studying each candidate and examining (his or her, their) political views.

_____ 15. Were any of the cars parked in (its, their) assigned parking spaces?

_____ 16. Keep your parakeet out of drafts; (he, it) can easily become chilled.

_____ 17. Both of the drivers foolishly insisted on defending (his, their) right of way.

_____ 18. In my opinion, neither of the candidates clearly enunciated (his, their) views during the debate.

_____ 19. None of the paintings belong to (its, their) original owners.

_____ 20. Somebody has left (his, their) books in Room 310.

_____ 21. Did either of the girls who telephoned tell you what (she, they) wanted?

_____ 22. No one had done (his, their) homework!

_____ 23. Both Robert and Chris are going to express (his, their) opinions of the proposal.

_____ 24. Jeremiah was one of the Hebrew prophets who predicted the fall of Jerusalem in (his, their) prophecies.

_____ 25. The stallion led (his, its) mares to the high meadows in the spring.

Exercise 82: Degrees of Comparison

Give the comparative and superlative forms of these adjectives and adverbs.

		comparative	superlative
1.	big	_____	_____
2.	hopeful	_____	_____
3.	tremendous	_____	_____
4.	long	_____	_____
5.	vivacious	_____	_____
6.	foolish	_____	_____
7.	wacky	_____	_____
8.	loudly	_____	_____
9.	coarse	_____	_____
10.	fine	_____	_____
11.	mighty	_____	_____
12.	brave	_____	_____
13.	humorous	_____	_____
14.	pretty	_____	_____
15.	glorious	_____	_____
16.	famous	_____	_____
17.	sudden	_____	_____
18.	naive	_____	_____
19.	gloomy	_____	_____
20.	crisp	_____	_____
21.	critical	_____	_____
22.	crude	_____	_____
23.	much	_____	_____
24.	cautious	_____	_____
25.	well	_____	_____

Exercise 83: Using Adjectives and Adverbs

Correct any errors of adjective and adverb usage in these sentences. Add any additional words which may be necessary.

1. Which of these two paintings is the best example of chiaroscuro?

2. Of these five rolls of wallpaper, which fits the decor of our house better?

3. In my opinion, Heath plays more better than Dirk.

4. Is *Hard Times* the most shortest novel by Dickens?

5. Athens and Sparta were more powerful than any states in ancient Greece.

6. Howard can draw better than anyone in his art class.

7. The college bookstore doesn't have no more copies of *Antigone*.

8. I had not scarcely arrived at the hotel when I heard my name being called.

9. Senator Byrd of West Virginia is older than anyone in the Senate.

10. Yes, *Hamlet* is the most longest of Shakespeare's plays.

11. Which grow fastest, willows or oaks?

12. When I asked them why they had skipped class, they didn't say nothing.

13. I ran more faster yesterday than today.

14. *Measure for Measure* seems to be more allegorical than any of Shakespeare's plays.

15. The limestone formations in Mammoth Cave are the most strangest things I have ever seen.

16. According to this guidebook, Chartres is more beautiful than any cathedral in France.

17. Of all of Eliot's early poems, which seems to reflect his modernist views more accurately?

18. Is Madrid larger than any city in Spain?

19. Which of these three rugs is more appropriate for the dining room?

20. As you move to the third movement of the concerto, play more rapidlier.

21. Franklin Roosevelt shaped the modern Democratic Party more than anyone in the twentieth century.

22. We haven't got but one more box of these tee-shirts.

23. The Amazon is the most longest river in South America.

24. Which of the two gymnasts performed best on the parallel bars?

25. Which of these two exercises gave you the most trouble?

Exercise 84: Using the College Dictionary

Write the complete name of the college dictionary you are using for this exercise:

_____

Variant Spellings
Underline the spelling which your dictionary prefers.

1. Ashanti, Asante

2. Hanukkah, Chanukah

3. encyclopaedia, encyclopedia

4. tsar, czar

5. eon, aeon

Pronunciation
Write out the pronounciation of the given word, with any diacritical markings

6. inchoate _____

7. sibyl _____

8. hors d'oeuvre _____

9. Manichaean _____

10. xenophobe _____

Inflected Forms
Give the requested inflected form found in your dictionary.

11. What is the plural of *colloquy*? _____

12. What is the present participle of *deter*? _____

13. What is the plural of *innuendo*? _____

14. Give an adjectival form of the noun *sycophant*. _____

15. What is the past participle of *plot*? _____

Etymology
Write out the etymology which your dictionary gives for these words.

16. plumber _____

17. nascent _____

18. gladiolus _____

19. doom _____

20. banana _____

Synonyms
Give three synonyms of each word.

21. throw _____

22. exhorbitant _____

23. occurrence _____

24. propitious _____

25. ingredient _____

Idioms
Give the meanings of these idiomatic expressions.

26. to feather one's nest _____

27. to save one's breath _____

28. to break camp _____

29. to cast one's lot with _____

30. with flying colors _____

Scientific Information
Using your college dictionary, give the Latin genus and species names for each of these plants or animals.

31. China rose _____

32. onion _____

33. woodchuck _____

34. mistletoe _____

35. dog _____

Encyclopedic Information
Answer these questions using your college dictionary.

36. The Dixiecrats broke away from which political party? _____

37. Who was the twin brother of Romulus? _____

38. "Boss" Tweed controlled the political system of what city? _____

39. Brahma is a god in what religion? _____

40. What was the occupation of Paul Revere? _____

Exercise 85: Using the College Dictionary

Write the complete name of the college dictionary you are using for this exercise:

_____

Variant Spellings
Underline the spelling which your dictionary prefers.

1. sheikh, sheik

2. loath, loth

3. timpani, tympani

Pronunciation
Write out the pronounciation of the given word, with any diacritical markings.

4. fusilier _____

5. gules _____

6. novice _____

Inflected Forms
Give the requested inflected form found in your dictionary.

7. What is the plural form of *moose?* _____

8. Give the past participle of the verb *picnic.* _____

9. Give a noun form of the adjective *flagrant.* _____

Etymology
Write out the etymology which your dictionary gives for these words.

10. bloom _____

11. ostracize _____

12. sartorial _____

Synonyms
Give three synonyms of each word.

13. cherish _____

14. banish _____

15. palpable _____

Idioms

Give the meanings of these idiomatic expressions.

16. to earn one's stripes _____

17. to put one's foot in one's mouth _____

18. to bite the hand that feeds one _____

Scientific Information

Using your college dictionary, give the Latin genus and species names for each of these plants or animals.

19. apple _____

20. guinea fowl _____

21. raven _____

Encyclopedic Information

Answer these questions using your college dictionary.

22. In what year was John Thomas Scopes convicted for teaching evolution?

_____

23. Where did the Pequot Indians live?

_____

24. Who killed the Hydra in Greek mythology?

_____

Exercise 86: Restrictive Labels

Give the full name of the college dictionary you are using for this exercise:

_____

Give the restrictive label which your dictionary gives for each of these words.

1. phylactery _____

2. ground ball _____

3. Shabbat _____

4. repand _____

5. tyre _____

6. shoon _____

7. eftsoons _____

8. yardarm _____

9. allegro _____

10. caryatid _____

11. sine prole _____

12. sinter _____

13. swanny _____

14. doloroso _____

15. argent _____

16. holpen _____

17. methinks _____

18. you-all _____

19. cheerio _____

20. corpus delicti _____

21. neutral zone _____

22. fortissimo _____

23. pone _____

24. apse _____

25. imam _____

Exercise 87: Usage Labels

Give the full name of the college dictionary you are using for this exercise:

_____

Give the usage label (or any usage note) that your dictionary gives for each of these words.

1. rubberneck _____

2. schlep _____

3. ain't _____

4. humdinger _____

5. ritzy _____

6. rat race _____

7. popish _____

8. hoosegow _____

9. funny bone _____

10. gal _____

11. jiffy _____

12. henpeck _____

13. dorm _____

14. doodad _____

15. legit _____

16. irregardless _____

17. alright _____

18. pep _____

19. glad rags _____

20. amp _____

21. clobber _____

22. snot _____

23. nowheres _____

24. shiv _____

25. yes man _____

Exercise 88: Rhetorical Devices (Schemes)

In the blank at the left write out the name of a rhetorical scheme which is used in the illustration. Choose from one of the following: alliteration, anaphora, anastrophe, asyndeton, chiasmus, climax, ellipsis, parallelism, polysyndeton.

_____ 1. Slowly, silently, now the moon / Walks the night in her silver shoon. —Walter de la Mare

_____ 2. I have sent word to the president, and he to me.

_____ 3. We found them here and there and everywhere.

_____ 4. Blessed are the poor in spirit: for theirs is the kingdom of heaven. —Matthew 5:3

_____ 5. First we doubted the wisdom of the king's policies; then we questioned the rightness of his decisions. We remonstrated with him; we sent him petition after petition. We cautioned and warned him of our righteous anger. Finally, we declared him a tyrant and resisted him with manly force of arms.

_____ 6. I foamed, I raved, I swore. —Edgar Allan Poe

_____ 7. And the eyes of them both were opened, and they knew that they were naked; and they sewed fig leaves together, and made themselves aprons. —Genesis 3:7

_____ 8. In such a night as this, / When the sweet wind did gently kiss the trees / And they did make no noise, in such a night / Troilus methinks mounted the Troyan walls /And sighed his soul toward the Grecian tents, / Where Cressid lay that night. / ... / In such a night / Stood Dido with a willow in her hand / Upon the wild sea banks, and waft her love / To come again to Carthage. —William Shakespeare

_____ 9. My soul He doth restore again. —Psalm 23, *Scottish Psalter*

_____ 10. Never in the field of human conflict was so much owed by so many to so few —Sir Winston Churchill

_____ 11. Silent, mournful, abandoned, broken, Czechoslovakia receded into the darkness —Sir Winston Churchill

_____ 12. After the war, Western Europe, liberated from Nazi barbarism, marched into the light of liberty and free institutions. But from that light and away from that freedom, bound by Soviet chains, was dragged the pitiful East.

_____ 13. I must down to the seas again. —John Masefield

_____ 14. We shall fight on the beaches, we shall fight on the landing-grounds, we shall fight in the fields and in the streets, we shall fight in the hills. We shall never surrender. —Sir Winston Churchill

_____ 15. He shrank a little with his shoulders at the sharp iron. —*Sir Gawain and the Green Knight*

_____ 16. We hold these truths to be self-evident, that all men are created equal, that they are endowed by their Creator with certain unalienable rights, that among these are life, liberty and the pursuit of happiness. —Declaration of Independence

_____ 17. With all my worldly goods I thee endow. —Book of Common Prayer

_____ 18. We have left undone those things which we ought to have done, and we have done those things which we ought not to have done. —Book of Common Prayer

_____ 19. Glory be to the Father and to the Son and to the Holy Ghost.

Exercise 89: Rhetorical Devices (Tropes)

In the blank at the left write out the name of a rhetorical trope which is used in the illustration. Choose from one of the following: apostrophe, hyperbole, irony, litotes, metaphor, metonymy, onomatopoeia, oxymoron, paradox, personification, rhetorical question, simile, synecdoche, zeugma.

_____ 1. Our attempt to locate him has been a wild goose chase.

_____ 2. Their hisses grew louder by the minute.

_____ 3. Looking at the filthy room, his mother remarked, "What a magnificent job you have done! I trust you haven't overly exerted yourself!"

_____ 4. Our earlier critics were loudly silent.

_____ 5. Death, be not proud. —John Donne

_____ 6. "Which of you," asked the minister, "has not failed in some way?"

_____ 7. Thou shalt eat the labour of thine hands. —Psalm 128:2

_____ 8. He ran about like a chicken with its head cut off.

_____ 9. Strangely, if you search after happiness you will not find it; but you may stumble over it on the path of duty.

_____ 10. I could sleep for a year!

_____ 11. She always opened her door and her heart to the poor.

_____ 12. Proud-pied April, dress'd in all his trim, / Hath put a spirit of youth in everything. —William Shakespeare

_____ 13. The heaven is my throne, and the earth is my footstool. —Isaiah 66:1

_____ 14. This is no small problem.

_____ 15. Oh, my luve is like a red, red rose. —Robert Burns

_____ 16. He that is least among you all, the same shall be great. —Luke 9:48

_____ 17. You will always be welcome at my hearth.

_____ 18. Our veterans have laid aside the sword for more peaceful pursuits.

_____ 19. Like as the waves make towards the pebbled shore, /So do our minutes hasten to their end. —William Shakespeare

_____ 20. The Lord is my shepherd. —Psalm 23:1

_____ 21. Not a few of the emigrants died along the way.

_____ 22. The children smacked their lips in anticipation.

_____ 23. Milton! thou shouldst be living at this hour; / England hath need of thee. —William Wordsworth

_____ 24. Am I my brother's keeper? —Genesis 4:9

_____ 25. I will luve thee still, my dear, / Till a' the seas gang dry. —Robert Burns

Exercise 90: Glossary of Diction (1-10)

Using entries 1-10 in the Glossary of Diction, draw a line through any incorrect usage and write the correct wording above it. If a sentence is correct, write C to the left of the number.

1. Unfortunately, we are unable to except any further applications at this time.

2. The phone rang about 2:00 AM and woke me up.

3. Everyone accept Rachel was present today.

4. Due to the averse weather conditions, the meeting has been postponed.

5. Is the president averse to increasing the size of the budget deficit?

6. It will be difficult to gauge the affect of the presidential debate.

7. To affect a change in public attitudes, you must first change private values.

8. The extended low temperatures this spring have negatively effected crop yields.

9. She ain't the store manager.

10. Cromwell's phrase "the howling wilderness" is an allusion to Deuteronomy 32:10.

11. It is simply an allusion to think that you can live on credit indefinitely.

12. Did you do alright on the grammar test?

13. Lots of students have been absent this week with a stomach virus.

14. The acreage was divided between the four heirs.

15. Jane and I split a chocolate milkshake between us.

16. These french fries contain an incredibly large amount of fat.

17. Which candidate got the largest amount of electoral votes?

18. Weeks after the hurricane, a lot of trash was still piled along the streets.

19. Is your father adverse to your getting a part-time job?

20. Ain't he the captain of their team?

21. The weather can have a large effect on our feelings.

22. How will the high fuel prices effect automobile purchases?

23. You look quite pale. Are you all right?

24. A mirage is an illusion caused by the refraction of light by the heat.

25. Did you see an ad for these shoes in the newspaper?

Exercise 91: Glossary of Diction (11-20)

Using entries 11-20 in the Glossary of Diction, draw a line through any incorrect usage and write the correct wording above it. If a sentence is correct, write C to the left of the number.

1. His credit card debt last month amounted up to over $800.

2. I was not anxious to become involved in the matter.

3. His mother became somewhat anxious when she did not hear from him.

4. I looked for my history notebook everywheres.

5. Jackson feels very badly about what he said earlier.

6. Being as the hour is so late, I think we should leave now and start again tomorrow morning.

7. A large totem pole stands besides the entrance to the museum.

8. Where did you go in Alaska beside Anchorage?

9. It is cold tonight; you better wear a coat.

10. Between you and me, I think that was a bad decision.

11. At the very least, the physician's actions amount to misfeasance.

12. Anxious to get the mail, Susie waited on the porch for the mailman.

13. The inspectors could not find the weapons anywhere.

14. As the weather was bad, I decided to stay at home.

15. These prices seem awfully high to me.

16. The chemotherapy left him feeling quite badly.

17. Besides mowing the yard, Mr. Page also weeded the flower beds.

18. They were terrible angry about the situation.

19. Have you been able to locate a copy of the novel somewheres?

20. Being since my time is limited, I have to keep to a very tight schedule.

21. You had better finish reading the play tonight.

22. Between you and I, he looks rather sloppy.

23. A row of cedars stands beside the northern boundary of our property.

24. We were awfully sad to hear about his illness.

25. Does she feel badly about what she said to Diana?

Exercise 92: Glossary of Diction (21-30)

Using entries 21-30 in the Glossary of Diction, draw a line through any incorrect usage and write the correct wording above it. If a sentence is correct, write C to the left of the number.

1. There were a bunch of errors in his manuscript.

2. Can we borrow your step-ladder?

3. His thesis centered around the causes of World War I.

4. It is important to site any work that you quote or even borrow ideas from.

5. Our house is on the cite of a Revolutionary War battle.

6. My sister was totally disinterested in the baseball game.

7. A disinterested arbitrator can be called in to mediate the negotiations.

8. My father he was born in Virginia.

9. The senator's assertions illicited objections from several of his colleagues.

10. Dogs are frequently used to search for elicit drugs hidden in automobiles.

11. Mr. Schmucker's ancestors immigrated from Germany in the early eighteenth century.

12. Many Scotch-Irish emigrants to our country settled in the Appalachians.

13. An eminent pianist will be performing with the symphony next week.

14. The day when we must start paying back our student loans is now eminent.

15. I expect you are going to need a new transmission.

16. Mrs. Richards is expecting her son and daughter-in-law tomorrow.

17. A large bunch of robins descended on our front yard.

18. First, prepare the site by tilling the soil thoroughly and adding some compost or other organic material.

19. The illicit dealings of several of the leaders of the corporation resulted in four arrests.

20. The original immigrants to Australia were from Great Britain.

21. Professor Caruthers is imminently qualified to serve on the committee.

22. My father suspects that the water is coming from a loose pipe fitting.

23. Really, Sam is disinterested in art, but he went to the museum in order to spend some time with Kathy.

24. Almost all the French Protestants, called Huguenots, immigrated from France in the seventeenth century.

25. After the French and Indian War, the American Colonies they were gradually alienated from the British crown.

Exercise 93: Glossary of Diction (31-40)

Using entries 31-40 in the Glossary of Diction, draw a line through any incorrect usage and write the correct wording above it. If a sentence is correct, write C to the left of the number.

1. After redistricting, there were several thousand less voters in our precinct.

2. Ben did good on his algebra test.

3. Mrs. Martin has not been well for some time; she suffers from diabetes.

4. If he had of asked, I would of been glad to help him.

5. Pete had ought to graduate next year.

6. Hopefully, the electricity will be on by the end of the day.

7. Seven cars were involved in the accident; thankfully, no one was seriously hurt.

8. In his letter to me, Jared inferred that he may be moving soon.

9. From what my builder said, I implied that the cost may be higher than I had thought.

10. Joel ran in the office and asked to see the manager.

11. Outside of the Supreme Court were several groups of protestors.

12. Irregardless of the cost, we must have a new heating system in the classroom building.

13. Later in the afternoon, I began to feel kind of sick.

14. Inside of the court building was a large monument to the Ten Commandments.

15. Which has less calories, yogurt or cottage cheese?

16. Emily sings really good, doesn't she?

17. I wish we could of finished the painting today.

18. By observing the order and design of the universe, we can infer that it must of had an intelligent Creator.

19. "Would you like to go with me to the basketball game?" James asked hopefully.

20. I think this sofa is sorta large for our living room.

21. Susannah responded thankfully to Mrs. Little's job offer.

22. We must do the right thing, irregardless of the consequences.

23. The president's office is now located inside of the west wing of the White House.

24. Foods will have less fat when they are baked or broiled rather than fried.

25. Thankfully, the book I needed was not checked out already.

Exercise 94: Glossary of Diction (41-50)

Using entries 41-50 in the Glossary of Diction, draw a line through any incorrect usage and write the correct wording above it. If a sentence is correct, write C to the left of the number.

1. What kind of a bird has a black body with a red head?

2. Tyler was learned how to weld by his Uncle Dave.

3. It looks like it may snow this afternoon.

4. The beagle looks much like the foxhound.

5. Emma tried to sew the hem just like her mother had shown her.

6. Did you loose your umbrella again?

7. The doorknob on the basement door is loose.

8. After taking this medication, you may become somewhat nauseous.

9. The stone wall was pretty straight.

10. Her chicken and dumplings is real good; you should have some.

11. One reason for the English Civil War was because King Charles I wished to reduce the power of Parliament and emphasize his own royal prerogative.

12. Sharon and myself attended a workshop on money management.

13. How can you not enjoy the sensual beauty of a autumn day in the mountains?

14. In my opinion, the sensuous music of that song—not to mention the vulgar lyrics—make it inappropriate for anyone who cares about personal chastity.

15. What sort of parent would allow his children to be ill-fed?

16. Her grandmother learned her how to crochet, embroider, and knit.

17. I cannot forget the nauseous sight of the injured bodies and the twisted metal.

18. Heath invited Joanna to go with himself on a picnic.

19. The nest of the Baltimore oriole is real odd: it is woven out of grass and hangs from a tree branch like a small sack.

20. The reason for much of the unrest in the 1960s was because the values of the traditional culture were being widely rejected, with little regard for the consequences.

21. He would loose his head if it were not attached to his shoulders!

22. Our apartment is pretty small: it contains only five hundred square feet.

23. Do you feel like you have a fever?

24. After attaching the tag to the pheasant's leg, the game warden loosed it and set it free.

25. The students in the class attempted to sketch the bowl of fruit like Mr. Phillips had shown them.

Exercise 95: Glossary of Diction (51-62)

Using entries 51-62 in the Glossary of Diction, draw a line through any incorrect usage and write the correct wording above it. If a sentence is correct, write C to the left of the number.

1. I think this house is some larger than the one we looked at this morning.

2. My father was sure angry over my low grades.

3. The man which asked the question is a reporter for our local newspaper.

4. Move them papers off the chair and sit down, Jenni.

5. These kind of birds make nests on the ground.

6. Please, son, try and bring up your grade in trigonometry.

7. Who was the surgeon that operated on her?

8. Are them the roses that you planted last spring?

9. The little boy wanted off the roller coaster and began to scream.

10. We walked a long ways in search of a mechanic.

11. Where are they moving to?

12. Irony is when you use words to express the opposite of their literal meaning.

13. What is February like here, weather-wise?

14. Without you have read the play we cannot discuss it.

15. He is some stronger today; he is on the road to recovery.

16. A double play is where two players are put out in the same play.

17. Your home is sure pretty, Mrs. York.

18. Do those sort of cows produce much milk?

19. Try and straighten up the house before our guests arrive.

20. When the cat wants out, it sits next to the front door.

21. Them paintings are from the Impressionist period.

22. It is only a short ways from our house to theirs.

23. Is that the dress that you bought yesterday?

24. Them are the trees my father set out when we first moved here.

25. Where are you going to? Sit back down, young man!

Exercise 96: Capitalization

Circle all letters that should be capitalized.

1. The three planets nearest the sun are mercury, venus, and earth.

2. The city of nashville is located on the cumberland river in tennessee.

3. In the may issue of the *national geographic* there is an article about the amish of southeastern pennsylvania.

4. First-century jews often memorized large passages of the torah; it is not surprising that jesus' disciples would be able to quote him at great length in the new testament.

5. My father put a new set of michelin tires on our ford truck.

6. We went to the sylvan park restaurant, which is located at the corner of murphy avenue and forty-sixth street.

7. After the romans had evicted their last etruscan king, they set up a republican government.

8. In order to protect our democratic way of life, it is important that we maintain civilian control of such bodies as the fbi and the cia.

9. Consult frank owsley's book *plain folk of the old south* for a description of traditional southern life and culture.

10. Recently, our church got a new pastor, rev. donald m. douglas, sr.

11. The uygurs are an interesting people in western china: they are predominantly muslim and speak a language which is actually related to the european languages.

12. The first roman catholic settlers in the english colonies of north america arrived in 1634 on board two ships appropriately named the *ark* and the *dove*.

13. Beside the river of babylon, the psalmist exiled from judah cried, "if i forget thee, o jerusalem, let my right hand forget her cunning."

14. To get to chattanooga, go east on highway 40.

15. The sons of confederate veterans placed a wreath on the grave of jefferson davis, the president of the confederate states of america.

16. The students in ancient history 101 went on a field trip to centennial park, where there is a replica of the parthenon, the temple of athena in ancient athens.

17. The order of the cincinnati is made up of male descendants of officers who served with general george washington in the revolutionary war.

18. In 1215, king john signed the magna charta at runnymede near the thames river; that famous document limited the power of the british monarch.

19. Several of shakespeare's plays are set in ancient rome, for example *coriolanus* and *julius caesar.*

20. Ralph waldo emerson's famous poem "concord hymn" contains these lines describing the site of the battle of lexington and concord: "by the rude bridge that arched the flood, / their flag to april's breeze unfurled, / here once the embattled farmers stood / and fired the shot heard round the world."

Exercise 97: Capitalization

Circle all letters that should be capitalized.

1. Many muslims throughout the world study the koran, which is based on the teachings of mohammed.

2. A reporter from the *new york times* said, "will you support these substantial changes to the irs, senator?"

3. The astronauts in *apollo 11* were the first humans to walk on the moon.

4. Our pastor ended his sermon by praying, "teach us, i pray, o lord, to love you as we ought and then to love our neighbors as ourselves."

5. The civilization of the west grew out of the christian worldview, which was shaped by the hebraic culture of the bible and the hellenic culture of the playwrights and philosophers of greece.

6. In the summer of 2004, zell miller, the former democratic governor of georgia, made a rousing speech at the republican national convention in which he deplored some of the recent political positions of his own party.

7. "Get a jar of hellmans mayonnaise and a bag of sunbeam hot dog buns," said my mother, "and, oh yes, don't forget to purchase some bryan weiners."

8. The russian novelist fyodor dostoevsky examined the basis of human guilt in his profound novel *crime and punishment.*

9. In the elizabethan period, named after queen elizabeth i, england attained a high culture, which was the direct result of the european renaissance and the protestant reformation.

10. The city of new orleans lies between lake pontchartrain and the mississippi river; breaches in its levees caused severe flooding from both.

11. Do you know these lines from robert penn warren's poem "bearded oaks"? "we live in time so little time / and we learn all so painfully / that we can spare this hour's term / to practice for eternity."

12. Next winter there will be an exhibit entitled "the art of politics" at the national academy of art in washington, d. c.

13. At the battle of hastings in 1066, the duke of normandy and his french-speaking normans defeated harold and the english.

14. The island of bermuda, located about six hundred miles east of cape hatteras in the north atlantic, was first colonized by english settlers whose ship the *sea venture* was shipwrecked there on its way to jamestown, virginia, in 1609.

15. Later, shakespeare used this event as the basis for his play *the tempest,* which—curiously—has various references to the new world.

16. The marriage of prince charles and lady diana spencer, which began so beautifully on a june morning in st. paul's cathedral in london, eventually ended quite tragically and quite sadly.

17. At the recent funeral of the widow of king george vi, the archbishop of canterbury based his homily on this passage from proverbs 31: "strength and honour are her clothing; and she shall rejoice in time to come."

Exercise 98: End Marks

Add all necessary end marks.

1. Stop that man He stole my purse

2. Why was NATO formed after World War II

3. The guest lecturer in biology class was Ewell Brown, Ph D

4. Which corporate conglomerate recently purchased ABC

5. Please give your registration form to either Mrs Andersen or Miss Bradley

6. The new college president is Rev J Matthew Pinson, B A , M A , M A R

7. Are there any members of OPEC outside the Middle East

8. Dr Hester spoke to us about the origin of the New Testament

9. Which countries are permanent members of the UN Security Council

10. Donald Richardson, M D was recently named as the new county coroner.

11. Do you know our neighbor Mr Gonzalez

12. I believe it was CNN which first began offering news twenty-four hours a day

13. Have you met my pastor, Rev Paul Dickson, M Div

14. What do you think is the cause of this rash, Dr Knowles

15. Pass me the salt please

16. One of the good things about "The Jim Lehrer News Hour" on PBS is the extensive and thoughtful interviews

17. Which director of the CIA later became president

18. The later poetry of T S Eliot reflects the marked change in his thinking after his conversion to Christianity

19. How beautiful you look today, my dear

20. What was the original purpose of the FBI

21. The chairman of the company's board of directors is Howard Stone, Jr

22. F Scott Fitzgerald's novel *The Great Gatsby* explores the growing materialism and ethical confusion of the twentieth century

23. Is your lawyer named Phillip J Knight, Sr

24. Have you read the science fiction trilogy by C S Lewis

25. The speaker expressed his concern about the perceived bias of the news programming on NPR

Exercise 99: Commas

Add all necessary commas. If a sentence needs no commas, write C to the left of the number.

1. On Wednesday we will review chapter three and our test on verbs will be Friday.

2. Tennyson Browning and Arnold were poets of the early Victorian period.

3. The old rocking chair gave the room a warm cozy feeling.

4. The day after they went their separate ways.

5. My sister Eileen did her internship at a large urban hospital in Chicago.

6. On your way home get a jar of crunchy peanut butter.

7. This novel which was written in 1827 reflects a growing nostalgia for the simpler and more traditional world of pre-industrial Britain.

8. The weather having gotten much colder we decided to postpone the picnic.

9. Do you remember the oak trees that once lined this road?

10. Paul encourages the church to worship with psalms hymns and spiritual songs.

11. The roses growing along the sidewalk in front of the house are an old heirloom variety.

12. The house that we are building will have a large spacious living room.

13. The cold dark night gave way to a glorious sunny morning.

14. Before eating the raccoon usually washes its food.

15. Although Dickens's novels are not realistic they do accurately reflect life in nineteenth-century Britain.

16. The founders of our country warned against the dangers of a standing army because they had seen the excesses of British imperialism.

17. Sharon took the jars out of the boxes while I arranged them on the shelves.

18. He that gathereth in summer is a wise son but he that sleepeth in harvest is a son that causeth shame. —Proverbs 10:5

19. Many daughters have done virtuously but thou excellest them all. —Proverbs 31:29

20. In the words of Shakespeare "They that touch pitch will be defiled."

21. We were expecting guests so I baked a chocolate cake and vacuumed the house.

22. All of the cars that had the defective brakes were recalled by the company.

23. The gentleman who introduced the senator described his long prestigious career in politics.

24. The kind young woman wiped the injured soldier's fevered brow.

25. What did you do with the money that your Uncle Ned gave you?

Exercise 100: Commas

Add all necessary commas. If a sentence needs no commas, write C to the left of the number.

1. No Mrs. Jenkins we do not have any bananas.
2. Shakespeare died on April 23 1616 in his hometown of Stratford.
3. Send your college application to 3606 West End Avenue Nashville Tennessee 37205.
4. His campaign was, in my opinion, rather disorganized; it seemed to lack focus and intensity.
5. Then Christopher replied "That's not a very good reason."
6. On the contrary you will soon discover I believe that this is an unwise decision.
7. Good literature continually read for pleasure must let us hope do some good to the reader. —A. E. Housman
8. In quietness and in confidence shall be thy strength. —Isaiah 30:15
9. In her memoir *Cross Creek* Marjorie Kinnan Rawlings says "We cannot live without the earth or apart from it."
10. You may write to Senator Crawford at 1700 Monroe Street Tallahassee Florida 32419.
11. All things considered I think we did the best we could.
12. Behold how good and how pleasant it is for brethren to dwell together in unity! —Psalm 133:1
13. Despite our best efforts we lost the game.
14. Could you tell us Mr. President what your primary objectives are for your second term?
15. "Tell the truth and shame the devil" my grandmother always says.
16. According to his autobiography he was born in Mississippi.
17. If you wish to discuss your research paper with me you may come by my office.
18. Studying another language is frequently the best way of learning your own.
19. Yes sir I shall be here on Tuesday.
20. When asked whether he had broken the pitcher, little Willy tearfully replied "Yes ma'am I did but I didn't mean to."
21. Yesterday December 7 1941 a date which will live in infamy the United States of America was suddenly and deliberately attacked by naval and air forces of the empire of Japan. —Franklin D. Roosevelt
22. "Doug please give me your full attention" prompted Miss Sullivan.
23. Throughout the garden were large beds filled with tulips daffodils hyacinths and irises.
24. Because I could not stop for Death he kindly stopped for me. —Emily Dickinson
25. How we can best safeguard our country from terrorism was the primary question in the days after September 11 2001.

Exercise 101: Commas

Add all necessary commas. If a sentence needs no commas, write C to the left of the number.

1. A fool despiseth his father's instruction but he that regardeth reproof is prudent. —Proverbs 15:5

2. Eliot referred to such seventeenth-century poets as John Donne Andrew Marvell George Herbert and Thomas Traherne as the "metaphysical poets."

3. Having finished picking all the corn we lay down on the front porch for a good long rest.

4. Prior to painting Mr. Allen scraped off the old flaking paint and applied primer to places where the paint was missing.

5. Within our greenhouse grow bromiliads orchids poinsettias and other tropical flowers.

6. While I did not agree with everything that the candidate stood for I did agree with him on the most weighty matters so I voted for him.

7. As my father used to say "Half a loaf is better than no loaf at all."

8. After defeating his enemy Caesar wrote the Senate: "I came I saw I conquered."

9. Well although we cannot eliminate poverty we can of course do something to help the poor.

10. The Irish playwright Samuel Beckett spent many years in France and even wrote his most famous plays in French.

11. Senator may I ask you a couple of questions about your recent comments on television?

12. The beautiful young maiden who offered to water Eliezer's camels was Rebekah.

13. On the night before I wrote a letter to each of them explaining my sudden departure.

14. As a result of their customary and habitual use of firearms our troops tended to be better skilled in marksmanship.

15. My grandfather began his teaching career on September 10 1962 and he continued teaching until his retirement on May 30 2003.

16. Jared what do you and Emma think we should do to celebrate his retirement?

17. The most important political issues right now it seems to me are matters which will determine whether or not we remain a Judeo-Christian culture.

18. Should we for instance abandon the traditional view of human sexuality a position which has been taught for practically six thousand years?

19. During my holiday you may reach me at my cousin's home: 6921 North Highway 84 Andalusia Alabama 36420.

20. "They that can give up essential liberty to obtain a little temporary safety" said Benjamin Franklin "deserve neither liberty nor safety."

Exercise 102: Semicolons

Add all necessary semicolons. Change any incorrect commas to semicolons.

1. Savannah, Georgia, Charleston, South Carolina, and Williamsburg, Virginia are three old Southern cities that date from colonial times.

2. Now abideth faith, hope, charity, these three but the greatest of these is charity. —1 Corinthians 13:13

3. By the rivers of Babylon, there we sat down yea, we wept, when we remembered Zion. —Psalm 137:1

4. The hospital board of trustees consists of the following: David Smith, a local physician, Allen Page, a lawyer, Stephen Custis, the owner of an automobile dealership, and Eileen Figaroa, vice-president at Nelson Publishing.

5. Call your father at the office and tell him I'll be a little late, then pick up your sister from soccer practice.

6. The political situation in the Ivory Coast has deteriorated rapidly, consequently, all foreigners have been encouraged to leave the country.

7. Several members of the committee expressed their concern about the expenditure, however, the measure passed on a vote of five to four.

8. The desire of power in excess caused the angels to fall, the desire of knowledge in excess caused man to fall. —Francis Bacon

9. Pyrrhus was congratulated for winning a terrible battle, and he replied, "If we have another such victory, we are undone."

10. Bad men live that they may eat and drink good men eat and drink that they may live. —Socrates

11. The Graduate Record Examination will be given on Saturday, April 14, Tuesday, August 7, and Friday, October 28.

12. Life is very short and very uncertain, let us spend it as well as we can. —Samuel Johnson

13. The age of chivalry is gone, that of sophisters, economists, and calculators has succeeded. —Edmund Burke

14. We have had less rain this spring and summer, as a result, the apple crop this year is very meager.

15. Several older cities of the upper Gulf Coast (such as Pensacola, Florida, Mobile, Alabama, and New Orleans, Louisiana) were successively settled by the Spanish, the French, and the English, therefore, they have an interesting melange of cultures, seen especially in their cuisines.

16. Since the weather was beautiful, we took the afternoon off and went swimming, so we did not finish our chores until after dark.

17. In Cooper's novel *The Last of the Mohicans*, we find such interesting figures as Hawkeye, the intrepid woodsman, Chingachgook, the noble Mohican, Uncas, the young Mohican warrior, and Magua, the vengeful chief of the Hurons.

18. Many of the early lighter-than-air craft were unable to attain very high speeds, accordingly, they could not get sufficient lift to become airborne.

19. Wisdom crieth out she uttereth her voice in the streets. —Proverbs 1:20

Exercise 103: Colons and Dashes

Add all necessary colons and dashes.

1. The character of Washington is best summed up by these words from Henry Lee "First in war, first in peace, and first in the hearts of his countrymen."

2. During our tour of London we will be visiting these important sites Buckingham Palace, the Tower of London, the British Museum, and the Houses of Parliament.

3. My teacher's advice certainly improved my reading comprehension I can now focus rapidly on the main idea of each paragraph.

4. In Genesis 4 9 Cain asks God, "Am I my brother's keeper?"

5. Please bring the following items with you a pillow, sheets, three changes of clothes, toiletries, and a flashlight.

6. Your flight to Anchorage leaves at 6 25 PM.

7. "The Luck of Roaring Camp," "The Outcasts of Poker Flat," and "The Idyl of Red Gulch" these short stories by Brett Harte helped establish the new genre of "the Western."

8. Later, with the invention of cinema and then radio and television, the Western became a staple of American popular culture consider such programs as "Bonanza," "Gunsmoke," and "The Rifleman."

9. The dangers of false education are best summed up by these words from Alexander Pope "A little learning is a dangerous thing; drink deep, or taste not the Pierian spring."

10. Pearl Harbor, Bataan, Guadalcanal, and Midway these famous names from the Pacific theater of World War II are now etched in the history of the nation.

11. We all remember Dr. Johnson's regular admonition in chapel "If you'll sleep through chapel, you'll sleep through life!"

12. Etouffe, shrimp gumbo, jambalaya these classic Creole dishes became favorites of mine during my years in New Orleans.

13. To make this delicious etouffe you will need the following items onions, celery, bell pepper, garlic, and, of course, crawfish.

14. The effect of all those biscuits was obvious my pants were too tight, and my coat would not button.

15. My pastor ended his sermon by pausing dramatically and then quoting Galatians 6 7 "Whatsoever a man soweth, that shall he also reap."

16. From 1 30 until 4 45 Jan Karon will be at Davis-Kidd Bookstore, signing copies of her latest novel.

17. The Roman authors to be studied in this course will be as follows Vergil, Ovid, Catullus, and Horace.

18. *To Serve Them All My Days* is an excellent book for the future teacher it will give you an appreciation for the pleasures and pains of teaching.

19. In Genesis 5 1-32 you will find references to Seth, Enoch, Methuselah, and Noah.

Exercise 104: Parentheses and Brackets

Add all necessary parentheses and brackets.

1. For many years Strom Thurmond R., SC was the oldest member of the United States Senate.

2. Ivory Coast also known as Cote d'Ivoire has been the source of much instability in West Africa recently.

3. Dickens says, "He Scrooge became as good a friend, as good a master, and as good a man as the good old City knew."

4. The family tree of the houses of Lancaster and York see Appendix B is incredibly complex with numerous Henrys, Edwards, Richards, and Elizabeths.

5. Shakespeare presents King Richard III previously the duke of Gloucester as a physically and spiritually deformed monster.

6. The various physical effects of AIDS Acquired Immune Deficiency Syndrome are discussed in this pamphlet.

7. The humorous poems of Robert Service 1875-1958 frequently describe the life he discovered in the gold fields of the Yukon.

8. Giuseppe Masseria a.k.a. "Joe the Boss" was one of the early leaders of the Mafia in the United States.

9. The marriage of King Edward VIII and Mrs. Simpson even earlier Mrs. Spencer was unacceptable to the Church of England, to the royal family, and even to most of the king's subjects.

10. The period that came to be called the *fin de siecle* the "end of the century" was characterized by a sophistication that was empty of life and meaning.

11. The sphygmomanometer see illustr. 23 is used to measure the blood pressure.

12. The settlement at Londinium modern London was simply one of many Roman towns in Britannia.

13. The mistletoe *Phoradendron flavescens* is a parasitic shrub which can be found growing in the branches of other trees.

14. The murderous career of Billy the Kid William H. Bonney ended in an ambush in 1881.

15. Other passages cf. Romans 3:25 and 1 John 2:2 use the same Greek word.

16. The Federal Emergency Management Administration FEMA arrived in the storm-stricken city within three days of the hurricane.

17. In one of his poems George Herbert says, "A servant with this clause for thy sake makes drudgery divine." Is this attitude not the secret of contentment?

18. At the end of *Paradise Lost*, Milton pictures the scene this way: "They Adam and Eve hand in hand, with wand'ring steps and slow, through Eden took their solitary way."

19. The city of Salisbury in Latin Sarum was the home of the ancient kings of Wessex.

20. The destruction of Jerusalem A.D. 70 effectively ended the Jewish state.

21. His score on the SAT Scholastic Aptitude Test was quite high.

Exercise 105: Quotation Marks

Add all necessary quotation marks.

1. While going through the city Paul had seen an altar with the inscription To the Unknown God ; Whom therefore ye ignorantly worship, said Paul to the Athenians, Him declare I unto you .

2. O God, that men should put an enemy in their mouths to steal away their brains ! cries the drunkard Cassio.

3. Caesar's terse reply to the Roman Senate is famous: I came, I saw, I conquered .

4. Which American poet said, I have a rendezvous with Death ?

5. As a encore, Jessie Norman sang the beautiful old spiritual Nobody Knows the Trouble I've Seen ; then, after a moment's hush, the audience erupted in thunderous applause.

6. In his essay Of Studies, Francis Bacon remarked, Reading maketh a full man, conference a ready man, and writing an exact man.

7. In the chapter of *Moby Dick* entitled The Whiteness of the Whale Herman Melville discusses the symbolism of the whale's color.

8. Which Romantic poet wrote Ode on a Grecian Urn ? asked Dr. Howell.

9. Early in the service, the college choir sang the beautiful anthem If Ye Love Me , based on a text from the Gospel of John.

10. The historian J. R. Green described the effects of the English Reformation this way: England became the people of a book, and that book was the Bible. It was ... the one English book which was familiar to every Englishman.

11. I heartily recommend John Crowe Ransom's essay Reconstructed but Unregenerate , which treats the terrible effects of modern progressivism on American culture.

12. God bless us every one ! said Tiny Tim at the conclusion of the meager feast.

13. What doth the Lord require of thee, asked the Hebrew prophet Micah, but to do justly, and to love mercy, and to walk humbly with thy God ?

14. Was it Shakespeare who said, All the world's a stage ?

15. To be prepared for war, said President Washington, is one of the most effectual means of preserving peace .

16. Doug, said the minister, would you please lead us in a verse or two of Amazing Grace ?

17. According to *Grove's Dictionary of Music*, said Dr. Stevens, Mendelssohn's *Reformation Symphony* is based on Luther's hymn A Mighty Fortress Is Our God .

18. Are you familiar with the poem Jabberwocky by Lewis Carol? It begins, 'Twas brillig, and the slithy toves did gyre and gimble in the wabe .

19. Doesn't the expression tender is the night, which was used by Fitzgerald for the name of a novel, come originally from the poem Ode to a Nightengale by Keats?

Exercise 106: Italics

Underline any words, symbols, terms, or phrases which would be italicized in print.

1. There is an article in this week's issue of Time that discusses the terrible tsunami in Southeast Asia.

2. The destruction of the Lusitania by German u-boats contributed to America's entrance into World War I.

3. Whereas the word prophecy is a noun, prophesy is a verb.

4. Senator West showed that his opponent's defense of unlimited growth was wrong by means of a reductio ad absurdum.

5. In the play Death of a Salesman Willie Loman, the title character, grapples with the apparent emptiness and meaninglessness of his life.

6. You will notice in this handwriting sample that the writer frequently fails to cross his t's and x's.

7. A theme of memento mori is quite prominent in Everyman, the medieval English morality play.

8. When you were small didn't you learn the rhyme "i before e except after c or when sounding like a as in neighbor and weigh"?

9. The proper response to this problem will require some je ne sais quoi.

10. Rembrandt's etching Christ Receiving the Little Children is quite small, only about eleven by fifteen inches.

11. On the other hand, his painting The Blinding of Samson by the Philistines is a huge canvas, about seven by ten feet.

12. The amazing pictures sent back to earth by Huygens, the space probe sent by the European Space Agency, reveal startling images of Saturn's moon Titan.

13. Every time the name Savonarola appears in your paper you have misspelled it.

14. Have you ever noticed the way Europeans write the numbers 1 and 7?

15. After using the allegory effectively in The Pilgrim's Progress, Bunyan used it over and over, most notably in The Holy War and The Life and Death of Mr. Bad-man.

16. I'll Take My Stand, the Southern Agrarian manifesto written in 1930, raises serious questions about the wisdom of many so-called "progressive" ideas.

17. The best source for old English ballads (such as "Barbara Allen's Cruelty" and "St. George for England") remains Reliques of Ancient English Poetry, compiled in 1765 by Bishop Thomas Percy.

18. Have you ever heard anyone pronounce the word relevant as if it were spelled revelant?

19. Did you read that editorial by George Will in yesterday's New York Times?

20. In Paul Robert's mural Justice Lifts the Nations, the figure of Justice points with a sword downward toward a book on which is written "The Law of God."

21. James Watson, one of the discoverers of DNA, wrote an article in the Atlantic Monthly warning about the dangers of cloning.

Exercise 107: Hyphens

Add all necessary hyphens.

1. The recent pictures of Saturn's moon Titan reveal that it is a bright pumpkin orange color.

2. The fifty six signers of the Declaration of Independence risked their lives by signing it.

3. Is that a one way street?

4. Combine a one third cup of cream and three fourths of a teaspoon of cinnamon to the mashed sweet potatoes.

5. Two thirds of the forty seven paintings in our local art museum are nineteenth century American works.

6. It is clear from Khomeini's earliest statements (which are clearly anti American and anti Western) that he rejected the accepted views of the modern Western world.

7. In return, many modern Westerners view the neo Islamic regimes of the Middle East as nondemocratic and dangerous to freedom.

8. Do you think he will make it onto the all star team?

9. Self pity is a dangerous attitude that can result in all types of problems.

10. Augusto Pinochet, the ex general and ex president of Chile, was charged with abuses of power during his seventeen year term of office.

11. Traditionally, the president elect rides to the inauguration with the previous president; however, there are a few historical exceptions.

12. I thought that Sarah seemed quite self assured and confident during her speech.

13. What percentage of Israelis are non Jewish?

14. Two car garages are now considered standard in new homes.

15. Do coin collectors prefer newly minted coins or coins which have been in circulation for many years?

16. The woman and her two year old child were left homeless and destitute.

17. A bridge on Twenty fourth Street crosses the river and takes you to Edgerton, one of the city's earliest suburbs, an area of red brick two story houses.

18. The young chemist added thirty two milligrams of sodium to the solution containing sixteen milligrams of nitrogren.

19. Leave a one and a half inch border on the left side of your research paper; leave a one inch border on the other three sides.

20. It became clear that our trip to the city was going to be an all day affair; we would not arrive back home until well after dark.

21. The self confessed murderer was quickly found guilty by the twelve person jury and then sentenced to death by the presiding judge.

22. The seven to two decision of the Supreme Court in the case of *Roe v. Wade* was believed by many to be unconstitutional, as well as immoral and non Christian.

Exercise 108: Apostrophes

Add all necessary apostrophes and make any other changes necessary to make the sentences correct.

1. John Adams defense of the British soldiers on trial for the Boston Massacre is one of the shining moments in our countrys history of jurisprudence.

2. We read again the stirring words of Pericles funeral oration in which he praised Athens beautiful way of life.

3. For goodness sake, you boys come in out of the rain.

4. A large collection of womens clothing was delivered to the Union Mission.

5. Is the Schaeffers house on Bowman Street?

6. The cows stalls were arranged in an orderly row along the buildings east side.

7. My brother-in-laws car broke down again.

8. Daniel and Joannas new house will not be finished until the early summer.

9. David and Walters shoes were left on the back porch to dry.

10. If the groundhog sees it's shadow on February 2, they say that we will have six more weeks of winter.

11. Who's books are these on the dining table?

12. Someones coat was left hanging in the hall all week.

13. The large number of *and*s made the sentences excessively long and difficult to follow.

14. These repeated *c*s are an excellent example of alliteration.

15. I took seven shirt's to the laundry this morning.

16. The Great Depression in the 1930's caused great hardship throughout the nation.

17. You must work on your handwriting; your *m*s and your *n*s are indistinguishable.

18. We were invited to go along on Greg and her picnic.

19. Bob's and Clara's oldest son is in medical school in Baltimore.

20. If something is everybodys job it will wind up being nobodys job.

21. Davis's and Roberts's Hardware Store is one of the oldest business establishments in our town.

22. Isn't one of Jesus's parables about an unjust judge?

23. Which of these coats is her's?

24. Are these puppy's for sale?

25. The poems titles are taken from stories in classical mythology.

Exercise 109: Slashes

Use a quotation from one of these passages of poetry in a sentence, utilizing slash marks to indicate ends of lines of poetry. Write the sentence in the spaces provided.

1. I think that I shall never see
   A billboard lovely as a tree.
   Perhaps, unless the billboards fall,
   I'll never see a tree at all. —Ogden Nash

2. Why, all the souls that were, were forfeit once;
   And He that might the vantage best have took
   Found out the remedy. How would you be,
   If He, which is the top of judgment, should
   But judge you as you are? —William Shakespeare

3. Of Man's first disobedience, and the fruit
   Of that forbidden tree whose mortal taste
   Brought death into the world, and all our woe,
   With loss of Eden, till one greater Man
   Restore us, and regain the blissful seat,
   Sing heavenly Muse. —John Milton

4. I preached as never sure to preach again,
   And as a dying man to dying men. —Richard Baxter

5. The world is too much with us; late and soon,
   Getting and spending, we lay waste our powers:
   Little we see in Nature that is ours. —William Wordsworth

Exercise 110: Ellipsis Marks

Choose one of these quotations. Shorten it and use it in a sentence, utilizing ellipsis marks to indicate where you have omitted words. Write the sentence in the space provided.

1. To be of no church is dangerous. Religion, of which the rewards are distant, and which is animated only by faith and hope, will glide by degrees out of the mind unless it be invigorated and reimpressed by external ordinances, by stated calls to worship, and the salutary influence of example. —Samuel Johnson

2. I wish the bald eagle had not been chosen as the representative of our country; he is a bird of bad moral character; like those among men who live by sharping and robbing, he is generally poor, and often very lousy. The turkey is a much more respectable bird, and withal a true original native of America. —Benjamin Franklin

3. I do not know what I may appear to the world; but to myself I seem to have been only a boy playing on the seashore, and diverting myself in now and then finding a smoother pebble or a prettier shell than ordinary, whilst the great ocean of truth lay all undiscovered before me. —Sir Isaac Newton

4. Good name in man and woman, dear my lord,
Is the immediate jewel of their souls:
Who steals my purse steals trash; 'tis something, nothing;
'Twas mine, 'tis his, and has been slave to thousands;
But he that filches from me my good name
Robs me of that which not enriches him,
And makes me poor indeed. —William Shakespeare

5. We are the victims of a voracious technology, ruthlessly consuming the resources of the earth. A Pandora's box has opened which no one can close. Everyone realises that for all their benefits these things will bring about huge collective disasters. The march of progress has crushed gentler species of animal and plant to extinction beneath its feet. But the gentlest and rarest species are the creative gift of art and the fear of the Creator; both of which, speaking generally, have disappeared. —Quinlan Terry

_____

_____

_____

_____

_____

Exercise 111: Punctuation

Edit these sentences, indicating any changes necessary in their punctuation.

1. In his lecture today Dr Eddins spoke on the culture of first century AD Palestine.

2. We discussed the following poems by Robert Frost Mending Wall The Death of the Hired Man and The Gift Outright.

3. A twenty foot high wall of water came crashing down on the quiet idyllic village.

4. From Stettin in the Baltic to Trieste in the Adriatic an iron curtain has descended across the continent. Behind that line lie all the capitals of the ancient states of Central and Eastern Europe Warsaw Berlin Prague Vienna Budapest Belgrade Bucharest and Sofia. —Sir Winston Churchill

5. Behind their home was a large woodland garden large beds of azaleas were interspersed with pines dogwoods and yaupon also known as native holly.

6. Fyodor Dostoevskys novel The Brothers Karamazov which he finished shortly before his death presents characters which are searching for some type of salvation.

7. Death be not proud though some have called thee / Mighty and dreadful for thou art not so. —John Donne

8. The basilica a long narrow room with a high ceiling and a platform at one end was developed by the Romans for use as law courts however the early Christians took this architectural form and used it for their churches.

9. C S Lewis wrote concerning pain God whispers to us in our pleasures speaks in our conscience but shouts in our pains it is his megaphone to rouse a deaf world .

10. Donald what is the meaning of the Greek word psyche asked Mr McAffee.

11. In my opinion this mornings sermon raised a very good question where do self confidence and self reliance end and pride and self conceit begin

12. As a youth Vladimir Lenin studied in a Russian Orthodox seminary but he later became rabidly anti Christian and based his life on Marxist materialism.

13. Many of the eighteenth century buildings in Williamsburg Virginia have been restored or rebuilt.

14. In his woodcut entitled The Four Horsemen of the Apocalypse German artist Albrecht Durer depicted the powerful scene described in Revelation 6 1-8.

15. In his Exhaustive Concordance of the Bible Rev. James Strong lists all the words used in the English Bible he also gives their Hebrew and Greek originals.

16. Evangelism evangelist evangelical these and other related words derive from the Greek word evangelion meaning good news .

Exercise 112: Punctuation

Edit these sentences, indicating any changes necessary in their punctuation.

1. NATO was formed in the late 1940s as a defense pact against the Soviet Union it included the countries of Western Europe the United States and Canada.

2. The Star Spangled Banner was written by Francis Scott Key during the War of 1812 however it was not adopted as the national anthem until 1931.

3. Let me quote from Thomas Jefferson The God who gave us life gave us liberty at the same time .

4. The signers of the Declaration of Independence end that immortal document with this oath We mutually pledge to each other our lives our fortunes and our sacred honor .

5. Seventeenth century New York then called New Amsterdam was already a city of various nationalities.

6. The Virginia and Kentucky Resolutions see Appendix G raised serious questions about the newly formed government.

7. James Fenimore Cooper William Cullen Bryant and Edgar Allan Poe these were really the first widely read American authors.

8. After they had been at sea for sixty five days the settlers on the Mayflower landed on the rocky barren shore of Cape Cod.

9. The House of Burgesses the first example of representative self government in the New World was established in 1619.

10. Although he was from a humble origin William Bradford was a scholar he had taught himself to read Hebrew Greek Latin French and Dutch.

11. Solid hard working German settlers made up approximately one third of the population of colonial Pennsylvania.

12. Joel are you familiar with Robert Frosts poem The Gift Outright

13. When the Constitution was ratified there were still tax supported churches in three states Massachusetts Connecticut and New Hampshire.

14. In his famous spelling book Noah Webster removed the u s from such words as honour and colour and changed the spelling of words such as theatre to theater.

15. For this pumpkin pie you will need the following one cup of pumpkin three fourths of a cup of milk and one fourth teaspoon of allspice.

16. There was an article in yesterdays edition of the Nashville Tennessean concerning Davy Crockett the famous frontiersman and three time congressman.

17. According to Article V of the Constitution the approval of three fourths of the states is needed to amend the Constitution.

18. The states rights are pointed out in the Tenth Amendment see p. 443.

Exercise 113: Capitalization and Punctuation

Edit these sentences, indicating any changes necessary in their capitalization or punctuation.

1. The tune for the hymn thine is the glory is taken from the opera judas maccabeus by george frederick handel.

2. Such diverse views as freudian psychology and marxist economics are actually built upon the foundation of evolution that theory was put forth quite clearly in the origin of species published by charles darwin in 1859.

3. She quoted this statement from jesus sermon on the mount blessed are the meek for they shall inherit the earth.

4. The twenty seven books of the new testament begin with the four gospels matthew mark luke and john .

5. The marshall of this years independence day parade will be george douglas jr our state senator.

6. The two planets farthest from the sun are pluto and uranus they are over a billion miles from earth.

7. Last winter the northeast suffered a terrible series of blizzards resulting in over twenty three deaths.

8. Since she knew that i am going to college next fall, my mother bought be a new compaq personal computer for christmas.

9. An article in christianity today discussed the ineffective action of rowan williams the archbishop of canterbury in response to the growing schism in the american episcopal church.

10. Yes father david and my loan was approved yesterday.

11. A thorough examination of the remains of the etruscan house were done in situ before they were taken to florence for further study.

12. These paintings of luther and his wife illus. 8-9 were done by lucas cranach the german painter and engraver.

13. Commenting on the renaissance painting the adoration of the lamb francis schaeffer says van eyck comprehended the bibical understanding of christ as the lamb of god .

14. The dome of the cathedral was designed by brunelleschi but the bell tower was designed by giotto.

15. The new professor of art history is diana foster ph d she earned her doctorate at the university of toronto.

16. The dark fast moving clouds certainly seemed to threaten erics and mollys picnic.

17. The first floor rooms of the thigpen building which is named after the college's second president is used for various meetings and receptions.

18. We sometimes forget that the southwest was settled by the spanish at a very early date albuquerque new mexico for instance was founded in 1706.

19. At 8 00 PM the boston pops orchestra under the direction of keith lockhart will perform selections from bizets opera carmen.

20. She leaned out of a window and screamed the house is on fire

21. Forty seven years after his first visit general lafayette 1757-1834 returned to america and was entertained throughout the nation with receptions balls and parades.

22. Do not use &s in formal writing write out the word and.

Exercise 114: Abbreviations and Numbers

Edit these sentences, indicating any changes necessary in the use of abbreviations and numbers. If a sentence is correct, write C to the left of the number.

1. My calculus class, which meets 1st period, is taught by Dr. Joanna Etheridge, Ph.D.

2. Edward, VI was the youngest of the 3 children of Henry, VIII.

3. What did Rev. Wallace preach on this morning?

4. We were honored by the presence of the Hon. Bill Purcell, mayor of Nashville.

5. The 50th annual general session will convene on Tuesday, July 17, at 10:00 AM in the morning.

6. The last Roman emperor in the West died in four hundred seventy-six AD.

7. Darwin, Marx, Nietzsche, et. al. indeed produced a modern world, but it was a world without room for God.

8. The early Romantic poets (ie Wordsworth, Coleridge, and Keats) still spoke the old religious language of the past.

9. Their religious terminology (eg "God" or "the divine") now denoted new concepts far removed from the old orthodoxy.

10. 53 people were killed in the train wreck about two hundred miles north of Sacramento.

11. Out of 122 entries, my brother's painting came in 2nd.

12. Their wedding begins at 2 o'clock in the afternoon on June 3.

13. The chairman of the committee is Henry Mason Sr.

14. The Babylonians conquered Jerusalem and destroyed the Jewish temple in BC 586.

15. The invasion of the Anglo-Saxons (ca 450) marked the beginning of the end for the Celtic control of the island.

16. The invocation was given by the Rev. Walter Hansen, pastor of Trinity Lutheran Church.

17. The American presidents during the Cold War (i.e. Truman to Reagan) were forced to maintain a massive military in order to resist the Soviet threat.

18. Where would you find the 10 Commandments in the Bible?

19. The ship was over three hundred feet long.

20. 7,962 votes were cast for Senator Lawson in our county alone.

21. Will you be at home around October 17th?

22. The Hebrew prophets (Isaiah, Jeremiah, et al.) spoke out against the growing materialism and hedonism of their culture.

23. Did Paul write 12 or 13 epistles?

24. The Battle of Manassas (i.e., the Battle of Bull Run) was the 1st battle in the War Between the States.

25. Over fifty thousand American soldiers died in Viet Nam.

Exercise 115: Word Division

Rewrite these words, indicating by hyphens the places where they might be correctly and appropriately divided at the end of a line. If a word cannot be correctly divided, merely write the word again without a hyphen.

1. concerned   _____

2. renew   _____

3. evade   _____

4. superabundance   _____

5. passing   _____

6. marveling   _____

7. occurring   _____

8. governor-elect   _____

9. self-described   _____

10. Puccini   _____

11. anti-Semitic   _____

12. pan-American   _____

13. burned   _____

14. frozen   _____

15. spelling   _____

16. four-story   _____

17. Shakespeare   _____

18. antepenultimate   _____

19. submarine   _____

20. pole-vault   _____

21. premillennial   _____

22. Alexander   _____

23. impropriety   _____

24. impressive   _____

25. pealed   _____

Exercise 116: Sentences, Fragments, and Run-ons

In the blank at the left, tell whether the group of words is a sentence (S), a fragment (F), or a run-on (RO).

_____ 1. The novel which he wrote during his first year in California.

_____ 2. I presented the proposal which the committee had agreed upon, then I answered questions from the audience.

_____ 3. The gradual (howbeit small) increases in the average temperature as a result of the widespread use of fossil fuels.

_____ 4. Uncle Remus, the famous story-teller invented by Joel Chandler Harris.

_____ 5. After graduating from college with a degree in history, he taught for three years in western Kentucky, he later went to law school in Louisville.

_____ 6. The pipes along Central Avenue are being replaced; hence, the water will be off in a three-block area beginning at 7:00 AM.

_____ 7. At that time, girls and women in rural French villages frequently wore traditional coifs and dresses on Sundays and holidays.

_____ 8. One of the tasks of the English teacher is to instruct freshmen in the proper method of researching, writing, and preparing a term paper.

_____ 9. The police located several people who were present at the time of the incident, but they either did not see the crime occur or could not remember much about it.

_____ 10. During the long, cold days in the Alaskan winter.

_____ 11. I tried to arrange my schedule so that my classes were in the early morning, I find that I can concentrate better in classes before lunch.

_____ 12. First, you sew the pieces together in some pattern of your choice; next, you attach them to a cotton filler and a fabric liner.

_____ 13. On the contrary, that is a responsibility of the states not the federal government.

_____ 14. Have you read George Orwell's _Animal Farm_?

_____ 15. The work is a brilliant satire of the Communist revolution in Russia and the subsequent development of the Soviet totalitarian state.

_____ 16. To step out of the bright sunlight into the shade of orange trees; to walk under the arched canopy of their jadelike leaves; to see the long aisles of lichened trunks stretch ahead in a geometric rhythm; to feel the mystery of a seclusion that yet has shafts of light striking through it. —Marjorie Kinnan Rawlings

_____ 17. There were a few carrots that I hoped to bring through the heat, a few zinnias, half a dozen desperate collard plants, poor things but mine own. —Marjorie Kinnan Rawlings

_____ 18. Hope is the thing with feathers that perches in the soul and sings the tune without the words and never stops at all. —Emily Dickinson

_____ 19. Under the rafters of the old barn roof, in the loft usually reserved for loose hay.

_____ 20. The film was set in China during the Japanese occupation of the 1930s.

_____ 21. She was preoccupied with her thoughts, consequently, she burned the pie.

_____ 22. The secretary of state and the British foreign minister each gave a short speech, then they answered questions from reporters.

_____ 23. The workmen building the new house at the corner of Richland Avenue and Craighead Street.

_____ 24. A detailed study of the mollusks illustrated with amazing color photographs.

_____ 25. These are the times that try men's souls. —Thomas Paine

Exercise 117: Coordination

Edit these sentences, eliminating any errors in the use of coordination. Rewrite them in the spaces provided.

1. It was a large package and which was wrapped in brown paper.

_____

_____

2. I needed new spark plugs, and my engine was sputtering.

_____

_____

3. There had been a snowstorm and so the road was quite slick and so he stopped for the night.

_____

_____

4. The photocopier kept having paper jams, and Caroline called the technician again.

_____

_____

5. Dr. Lawson is a very helpful academic advisor and who always seems glad to talk to me.

_____

_____

6. David heard a noise and he went downstairs and he looked around.

_____

_____

7. He served as college president for ten years and during which time he oversaw the construction of a new library.

_____

_____

8. He had finished all his research, and he started writing his paper.

_____

_____

9. The patient's appendix was inflamed and so he was in a great deal of pain and so the doctor recommended immediate surgery.

_____

_____

Exercise 118: Subordination

Edit these sentences, eliminating any errors in the use of subordination. Rewrite them in the spaces provided.

1. He wrote a lengthy letter, which would explain his view of the matter, which was unfortunately rather confusing.

   _____

   _____

2. The colonists wanted a voice in their own government was the root cause of the American Revolution.

   _____

   _____

3. The reason for your low grade on your paper was because you did not have a clearly defined thesis statement.

   _____

   _____

4. On Tuesday, a chair which was made by my brother, who is an excellent craftsman, will go on display in an exhibit which will feature artists who live in the local area.

   _____

   _____

5. Nicholas II, who had been forced to abdicate the throne of Russia, which his family, who were called the Romanovs, had ruled since the seventeenth century, was brutally murdered by the Bolsheviks, who hoped to establish a Communist dictatorship.

   _____

   _____

6. The reason Doug did not do well on the quiz is he did not read the assignment.

   _____

   _____

7. In my opinion, the reason that he was turned down for the position is because he simply does not have any experience.

   _____

   _____

8. They rented an apartment which has only two bedrooms, which will not be large enough for them.

   _____

   _____

Exercise 119: Misplaced Modifiers

Edit these sentences, correcting any misplaced modifiers. Rewrite them in the spaces provided.

1. Hanging on a hook in the attic, he found his father's old briefcase.

_____

_____

2. My father said on Saturday we would be cleaning out the garage.

_____

_____

3. The roofers had by the time we got home finished removing the old shingles.

_____

_____

4. Be sure to thoroughly and completely fill out the application.

_____

_____

5. By the end of the afternoon I had only completed one of my assignments.

_____

_____

6. Diana found a first edition of a book written by Jack London in a box at a yard sale.

_____

_____

7. I could see a large flock of wild turkeys looking out over the field.

_____

_____

8. She told the children how the martyrs had been burnt at the stake in Sunday school.

_____

_____

9. I showed a book to my brother that was published in the eighteenth century.

_____

_____

10. Crawling down the dining room wall, she saw a large spider.

_____

_____

Exercise 120: Dangling Modifiers

Edit these sentences, correcting any dangling modifiers. Rewrite them in the spaces provided.

1. By exercising for only thirty minutes a day, your weight can be considerably reduced.

_____

_____

2. While sitting on the curb, my feet grew colder and colder.

_____

_____

3. Looking out the windows of the airplane, the Rocky Mountains could clearly be seen below.

_____

_____

4. To get the best performance from your engine, it needs regular maintenance.

_____

_____

5. Having missed four classes in a row, my history professor called me to come to his office.

_____

_____

6. When quilting, care should be taken to keep the stitches small and regular.

_____

_____

7. Saved from demolition, local citizens began work on the restoration of the eighteenth-century farmhouse.

_____

_____

8. To graduate in May, transcripts for all coursework taken at other colleges must be turned in by March 31.

_____

_____

9. The soldier's legs grew tired while on guard duty.

_____

_____

10. In order to play the piano well, practice is absolutely necessary.

_____

_____

Exercise 121: Pronoun Reference

Edit these sentences, correcting any errors in pronoun reference. Rewrite them in the spaces provided.

1. Donald had lunch with his Uncle Marvin three times while he was in Charlotte.

2. We took the dishes out of the boxes and put them in the storeroom.

3. Alice and Natalie talked all through class today, which really bothered Dr. Reid.

4. On my way to work this morning I ran out of gas; unfortunately, that put me in a bad mood all day.

5. When I was in college, my pastor encouraged me to pray each day; until then, that had not been a regular part of my life.

6. In the Renaissance they rediscovered the artistic concept of perspective.

7. Even now in Communist China you can be arrested for illegal religious activities.

8. Lee had served both as a general and as superintendent of West Point, which made him a good college president.

9. In this recipe, it says to soak the beans overnight.

10. My father and I go deerhunting every year, but neither of us has ever shot one.

Exercise 122: Parallelism

Edit these sentences, correcting any errors in parallelism. Rewrite them in the spaces provided.

1. The lecturer presented some techniques for composting, planting, and how to prevent weed growth.

_____

_____

2. Plato's dialogues include situations from Socrates' life and which raise important philosophical questions.

_____

_____

3. This dish can be made either with beef or turkey.

_____

_____

4. Interestingly, the Gospel writers have neither given a description of Jesus' physical appearance nor many events from His childhood.

_____

_____

5. Upon completing your research project, you will both prepare a formal research paper and an oral class presentation.

_____

_____

6. The snow seemed to be less of a problem for our team than our opponents.

_____

_____

7. The Basques can be found throughout the Pyrenees, both in Spain and France.

_____

_____

8. I came to believe that he was not telling me the truth and he was hiding something.

_____

_____

9. Not only did the Vikings plant settlements in Greenland but also on the North American mainland.

_____

_____

10. You can get to Chattanooga either by Interstate 24 or Highway 70.

_____

_____

Exercise 123: Clarity and Logic

Edit these sentences, correcting any errors in clarity or logic. Rewrite them in the spaces provided.

1. The registrar believes that this year's enrollment is going to be as much if not more than last year's.

2. When we took a poll we discovered that a few of the students were opposed but most were in agreement with the new parking regulations.

3. The Robbinses have spent a week in the mountains every summer for many years, and they will again this summer.

4. Upon inspecting the work, I discovered that the brakes were still not repaired nor the oil changed.

5. We must have a genuine concern and interest in the needy in our community.

6. One of nine children, Lester worked his way through college as a gardener.

7. Born into an old Roman family, Julius Caesar virtually destroyed the old Roman republic and replaced it with a dictatorship.

8. In his famous novel *A Christmas Carol*, Dickens shows the reader Scrooge's indifference and unawareness of the massive problems of the poor.

9. Susan Kwai swam in yesterday's one-hundred-meter contest, but she won't in the three-hundred-meter race today.

Exercise 124: Unnecessary Shifts

Edit these sentences, correcting any errors caused by unnecessary shifts. Rewrite them in the spaces provided.

1. At first, Achilles is an incredibly proud man, willing for others to suffer as long as he prospers; but by the end of the epic he became more humane.

2. The Student Council has asked President and Mrs. Pinson to join them at their annual picnic.

3. If my father were here and was confronted with this problem, I think I know what he would do.

4. The guards may not have seen what was going on, but surely something was heard by them.

5. If one will drill the vocabulary words for about thirty minutes a day, you can master them relatively painlessly.

6. The letter from the bank said that I was overdrawn and would I get in touch with them immediately.

7. The mayor has promised to address the recent increase in burglaries; he insists that he is going to get these crooks off the street.

8. The little woman turned around, got into a karate stance, and knocks the mugger to the ground.

9. Bill's parents asked that he telephone them and lets them know if he is going to be late.

Exercise 125: Sentence Effectiveness

Edit these sentences, correcting any errors of sentence effectiveness (fragments, run-ons, coordination, subordination, misplaced modifiers, dangling modifiers, pronoun reference, parallelism, clarity and logic, and unnecessary shifts). Rewrite them in the spaces provided.

1. His flight from Phoenix was an hour late, consequently, he missed his connecting flight in Atlanta.

   _____

   _____

2. Hanging across Main Street, we saw a large banner welcoming us back home.

   _____

   _____

3. Emily telephoned Susan three times while she was out of town.

   _____

   _____

4. It was a beautiful poem and which expressed my thoughts almost perfectly.

   _____

   _____

5. Thousands upon thousands of stars, each millions of miles away.

   _____

   _____

6. Until quite recently, the wolf was almost extinct not only in Wyoming but also the other Western states.

   _____

   _____

7. My sister and her family have visited us every Christmas for the last five years, but this year they won't, because of financial concerns.

   _____

   _____

8. I wanted the book but it was quite expensive and I was already over my budget for the month.

   _____

   _____

9. The reason I gave you a failing grade is because you had two quotations that you did not cite at all.

   _____

   _____

10. My roommate stays up to all hours listening to music, which keeps me awake.

_____

_____

11. To be honest, I have neither serious concern nor even interest in this matter at all.

_____

_____

12. They bought a farmhouse which is old which is located on a dirt road which is in the southern part of the county.

_____

_____

13. In this brochure it says that azaleas need a very acidic soil.

_____

_____

14. By the end of the day the farmers had only finished reaping two of the fields.

_____

_____

15. Dr. Mancini spoke to the teacher education students about planning lessons, grading papers, and how to manage a classroom.

_____

_____

16. At first Bilbo was quite reluctant to go with Gandalf and the dwarves, but he eventually proves himself to be a stout-hearted companion.

_____

_____

17. Not answering her repeated calls, my mother came upstairs to see what was keeping me.

_____

_____

18. Has the faculty asked the dean of students to meet with them concerning the recent rise in student absences?

_____

_____

19. While walking about the streets of Europe, for safety a money belt should be worn.

_____

_____

Printed in the United States
122070LV00003B/163-338/P